How To Sell In Any Economy

Stan Peake
Catherine Brownlee
Lee Cassells

Edited by
Elli Townsend

Praise for "How to Sell in Any Economy"

This is a very practical sales book! Lots of hands on advice, including fundamental principles of sales that work in any economy. A really great reference tool for new sales people who want to get up to speed fast, as well as seasoned sales professionals looking to freshen up their sales strategy. Great job!
- Nicole Jansen, Leadership and Business Coach, host of Leaders of Transformation podcast, Los Angeles, CA.

"...achieve a more credible, trustworthy, and effective salesforce for the future. The strategies outlined in How to Sell in Any Economy should be adopted by every business leader who wishes to be truly competitive in this New Economy.
- Steve Allan, FCA, ICD.D Chairman of the Board – Calgary Economic Development Alberta Order of Excellence – 2018

How to Sell in Any Economy gives you a clear road map to success. The key takeaways: know you customer needs and know yourself. YOU are in sales! Whether it's a robust economy or an economic downturn these sales techniques, strategies and processes will allow you to achieve your full sales potential. Consider this the All-Terrain Vehicle of sales books, it will get you through anything!
- Martin Parnell, the man who ran 250 marathons in one year; TEDx speaker, author, multi-Guinness World Record holder

As it explains in "How to Sell in Any Economy", your ability to perform under pressure, or in adverse situations, is contingent on your ability to go back to the basics and consistently execute proven sales strategies.

I own, and have read, numerous books on personal selling strategies; however, this is the first book that truly addresses the disconnect between what most sales training programs teach, and what I know is the 'real world'. If you are just starting out on your sales career or are motivated to go to the next level of performance, I highly recommend you read this book.
- Norm Friend, President, Franchise 101 Inc. Vancouver, British Columbia

I would advise every sales and non-sales professional alike to read "How to Sell in Any Economy". I have been in sales for 30 plus years, have attended many sales courses and read all kinds of books on closing ...... Lee & the team have nailed this book in the ways of being a solution provider and selling a solution from your heart and not slick sales techniques.
Professional sales people struggle sometimes with getting painted with the "Used car sales slickster" brush, however, when sales are looked at properly like in this book, you will see selling through a different set of eyes and feel awesome finding solutions for your prospective clients in whatever industry you are in.
- Mike Joseph, President, Sales & Business Development; In Charge Life and In Charge Payments. Vancouver, British Columbia

The beauty of this incredible book is that you could take the word "Sell" from How to Sell in Any Economy and replace it with the word "Serve". Many of us who are "service entrepreneurs" struggle with the idea of actually making money at what we do because it is in service to others. Peake, Brownlee and Cassells reframe the concept masterfully reminding us that it is perfectly fine to personally benefit when you are adding so much value to others.

- Steve Boyle, Founder, 2-4-1 Sports, Advisory Board Chair - National Association of Physical Literacy, Partner - Dorm Room Coaching and Counseling, West Hartford, Connecticut

"Anyone and EVERYONE involved in the sales process HAS to READ "How to Sell in Any Economy"... when people ask you, 'If you knew then what you know now, how would your life be different?" Well, if I had this book 20 years ago, I'd be WAY further ahead today! This is the resource I wish I had when I began my sales career journey."

- Dai Manuel, Fitness expert, coach, and entrepreneur, Vancouver, British Columbia

Dedication

We wrote this book for our tribe: entrepreneurs, business leaders, and sales professionals all over the world. The world needs the best version of you, and we want to do our part to unleash your brilliance!

We could not have written this book were it not for the mentors and great leaders in our lives, or our supportive friends and families. Your support allows us to do the work we have been called to do, and none of it would be possible without you.

Table of Contents

Introduction

Just what the world needs – another book on sales!

While we know there's certainly no shortage of books on how to sell – there are still thousands of companies struggling to meet their targets across the world. In our coaching and consulting practice, sales consistently ranks among the top one or two concerns among new clients.

In our experience, we find the gap between capability and performance has less to do with a lack of knowledge or skill, and more to do with inconsistent execution of sound fundamentals. There are also a variety of human factors we want to address.

Would you be motivated to sell insurance the day after a big breakup? How genuine do you think your rapport building questions are with your prospect if you have no idea how you'll pay your bills this month?

In *How to Sell in Any Economy*, we combine our 70 years of business expertise to help you and your sales team attract more qualified customers and help them with their unique challenges in the process. Through our thousands of hours of research, we've also discovered there is a significant disconnect between what most sales training programs teach and how customers buy. In short, we want to help grow your sales, career and business while you enjoy the process and stay true to who you are!

So, while there are thousands of books out there on how to sell, we're bringing you the first book that combines proven sales strategies with ways to understand who your ideal customer is, and who you are as a professional. We want to share with you what they want (from their mouths), and more successful ways to find them. We even cover how to optimize your physical and emotional states so that the best version of you shows up at every meeting, and your clients like and trust you before they sign on the dotted line.

Whether you're a sales representative, business development manager, business owner, or just starting your career, *How to Sell in Any Economy* will become a vital resource **you'll come back** to again and again as your secret weapon!

We wrote this book for you – enjoy!

PART ONE

KNOW THYSELF

Chapter One

Your values ARE your value proposition

"People don't buy what you do, they buy why you do it."[1] - *Simon Sinek*

In our recruitment practice, we invited the President and CEO of a major company to a lunch meeting. We didn't just discuss the contract or even the opportunity, but rather a great many topics. More specifically, one topic of discussion was that they were ready to add a Human Resources Manager to their team.

Interestingly, we had recently met with a very good candidate who would fit this role and was keen to leave her current position. We offered to make an introduction for both parties, and the client agreed. The client also asked what else we did in the world of work and how we make money. We said that we were, "Unicorn Wranglers (we helped our clients find the type of candidates they weren't sure existed)." He laughed and said that he had been looking for a "Unicorn" for his global operation for over six years. We said, "Perfect!" That will be a great example of how we make our money.

The client was very impressed that we were willing to make an introduction to a Human Resources Manager (whom he hired), without charging his company. We built full trust in two hours. We then received the search mandate for the "Unicorn", who happened to be located in Italy (which we found in four days!) and another four search mandates over the following year.

Rather than being hyper-focused on one deal, we built a relationship which led to five deals! We've since become lifelong friends and have even been introduced to his family.

The above story is just one example of **many we've experienced** through our different businesses. If a business can learn to focus on their customers' needs more than their own, they'll be able to take care of their own needs as well. In the above example, five times the revenue was achieved for a similar input of time and resources – just a different approach.

This approach can't be faked, and it can't be fast-tracked, but it can be learned and mastered by literally anyone! Our approach is called "win-win selling" and, while we might be the first to study the science behind it and give it a catchy name, we can assure you that successful people from all industries have been enjoying massive success with this approach since the barter system.

Like any other successful strategy, there are several **components**, or necessary conditions, to win-win selling. So, what is win-win selling, and how is it different than the hundreds of other approaches and thousands of other books on sales out there?

At the heart of it, win-win selling is;

- Relationship selling more than transactional selling ("I'm here to build a trusted relationship over time more than I am here to sell you 15 units today.").

- Customer need is the focus of the conversation rather than the sales opportunity ("How can I make your life easier?" rather than "This is why you need this product."). The sales person must genuinely care.[2]

- Questions are asked to understand the customer's need more than pitches are given to elevate interest.[2,3,4]

- Customer need (or pain point) is measured against provider value proposition (solution-based selling). A competent, confident advocate positioning their offering as the ideal solution to their target customers' pain points and needs. ("This is why I love my job; I get to help customers like you solve the exact problem you just described!").

- Trust is engendered through the process, especially when the salesperson follows up and follows through on what they said they were going to do ("Jack, I'm calling today to make sure you're happy with your new mountain bike. Have you been out on the trails yet?"). This is such a critical part of the process. According to HubSpot, only 3% of buyers trust sales representatives![5]

- Both parties genuinely have each other's best interests in mind; they want to see each other succeed ("Myra, I'm going to give you an extra business card. Call me if your computer ever breaks down, even if it's five years from now and you're not sure if your laptop is compatible with changing software.").

- The vendor inspects customers and is honest if they aren't a great fit, even going so far as to recommend an alternative that might be a better fit for their needs.[3]
- Being authentic. Win-win selling is not about being who you need to be to land the sale in front of you. Rather, it's about being who you are, so you can effectively achieve your sales targets and take care of the customers who connect with you and who you connect with.
- Balancing performance orientation (winning and hitting targets) with conscientiousness and humility.[4] Working hard to win, but playing by the rules and honoring customers' needs, is more important than win-at-all-costs.
- The vendor creates, over time, enough of a referral base that they no longer focus on lead generation because they have developed such trust they become the ONE CALL for their clients. Their clients in turn refer them more business anytime a friend, family member, or colleague mentions a need that they can support.
- Anyone can learn this approach if they are passionate about what they do and genuinely care about serving their customers.

So, who are you? What do you do? Why are you passionate about what you do? Who are your customers? How do you serve them? Why are you passionate about serving your customers?

The clearer your vision, values, careers goals, and motives the better you will be able to integrate the strategic and tactical advice you are about to read. The better you can do this, the more confident and authentic you will show up to every meeting, which builds and reinforces trust, fosters relationships, feels better and, not surprisingly, leads to more sales.

To help you be perfectly clear on who you are as a sales professional (and as a person) there are three exercises to complete before going forward. To have a deep purpose that is too important to walk away from, we are going to have you create (or revisit) your future Vision, your Core Purpose Statement, and your Core Values.

Setting Your Future Vision

Companies need to make money, and that's not a bad thing. The companies that prioritize profit over everything else, and the corporate greed stories we read about, are what puts a bad taste in customers' and values-based sellers' mouths. The best way to feel great about selling, and to avoid fearing or feeling like you're becoming the next evil tycoon, is to create an envisioned future state wherein you or your company have achieved profound success and positive impact in the world. Paint a picture of what you want your company (or career) to look like in 10 or 30 years.

Imagine you're at the most prestigious industry awards ceremony, where you (or your company or your team) are the recipient of the highest honor! What have you or your company done to deserve such an award? How have you made life better for your customers, team, and community?

14

Perhaps your vision is almost entirely altruistic and based solely in the enrichment of others' lives. Perhaps you're off the radar on the achievers' scale and your future vision is of complete and total industry dominance, achieved in an ethical way.

Spend some time in nature, or with the most uplifting people you know, and when your soul has been stirred and inspired, now is the time to think about what you hope to achieve as your Sistine Chapel or your Mona Lisa.

You may decide to read on, but don't go past chapter three until you have stirred your soul and written your ideal future vision. Go create your masterpiece!

Lastly, don't forget to include why this matters to you.

My ideal future vision is:

The reason this matters so much to me is because:

Uncovering Your Core Values

In our experience, most people have not gone through the exercise of uncovering what their Core Values are. It's important to note that everyone has values; however, not everyone is conscious of their values. Some people refer to their inner moral compass as their gut or their conscience; we call the three to five (for most people) absolute, non-negotiable moral must/must-nots your Core Values. It's important to differentiate a value from an ideal. A value is a filter that you actively use in your decision-making. If loyalty is a very strong value, you would not cheat on your spouse (especially if they were faithful), and you may even take loyalty too far and remain friends with those who aren't great friends to you. An ideal, however, is something that you aspire to, but do not act consistently in concert with. An extremely spontaneous person may aspire to one day be more organized, but they cannot claim

16

organization to be one of their values if they consistently live and act on the fly.

One of the best ways to uncover the values that are already inside of you is to select the five to ten values from the list below that most appeal to your inner core. Read the list below and circle, or highlight, the values you feel are most important to you and which you display consistently.

Select your top five to ten values from below and then move to the next exercise.

accountability	decisiveness	humility	personal growth
achievement	dialogue	humor/ fun	positive attitude
adaptability	ease with uncertainty	inclusiveness	power
ambition	efficiency	independence	pride
balance	embracing diversity	influence	professional growth
being liked	empathy	initiative	prosperity
being the best	enthusiasm	innovation	quality
caring	entrepreneurial	integrity	respect

caution	ethics	job security	responsibility
clarity	excellence	justice	reward
coaching/ mentoring	experience	leadership	risk-taking
commitment	fairness	listening	safety
community involvement	family	logic	self-discipline
compassion	fearless	making a difference	sincerity
competitive	financial stability	materialistic	team player
conflict resolution	forgiveness	mission focus	trust
continuous learning	friendship	open communication	vision
control	future generations	openness	well-being
cooperation	generosity	passionate	wisdom
courage	global awareness	patience	work ethic
creativity	health	perseverance	

curiosity	honesty	personal fulfilment

Narrowing the field

Now that you've selected at least five, and perhaps up to ten values, rank them. Compare each value side by side. if you had to choose, for example, between being honest, or being respectful (say of someone else's feelings), which value comes out on top for you?

When you've compared each value side by side, there will be a clear rank order to the values that you abide by and feel most strongly about. Also, there's no right answer. These are your values - we all have different experiences and influences; hence, we view the world differently. Order the values in the way that feels right for you.

Creating Your Core Purpose Statement

So now you've created the blueprint, or the intention at least, for your masterpiece and the values that make up your inner moral compass. You also had to answer why your future vision is important to you. The latter notion is a perfect segue into your Core Purpose. There is no bigger question than 'Why am I here?' (and you thought this was just a sales book!)

The reason that this is so important in sales, and in any profession, is that if we don't attach profound meaning to what we do and how we spend most of our time, we very quickly start to question the meaning of how we spend our days. If we conclude that what we do in any given day doesn't matter, it's a very fast downhill slide towards finding no satisfaction or joy in what we do, and then deciding to stop doing it altogether. Perhaps you've been there already – the existential crisis of asking what you were put on this earth to do, or why anything matters.

If we can understand and decide why we are here and why our important work matters, then we take much greater fulfillment and deeper meaning from attaining our goals and from successfully fulfilling our obligations.

Understand that just like coming up with a compelling future vision for yourself (or organization), defining your Core Purpose is deep work. It can be hard, and it can be messy. However, when you have it nailed (even the first version of what will evolve over time), a strong purpose has the power to drive your action and enhance the quality of your life. That being said, let's get to the heavy lifting!

What brings you deep joy?

Think back to the happiest two or three instances of your life (that aren't your wedding day or the day any of your children were born). What were you doing? Who were you with? Where were you? Why were these moments so special? Think on each of these and see if you can come up with some trends. If you can, these trends are the conditions of your happiness.

Perhaps Sarah remembers having a beer with her best friends after hiking a grueling mountain in Chile as one of these times. Even this simple example could teach her that the conditions of her happiness are;

- spending time in nature
- developing quality friendships
- challenging herself/ personal growth
- celebrating life
- delaying gratification (earning her beer)
- travelling and experiencing new places and cultures

So, let's put the concept to work for you.

My happiest moments that I can remember are:

The trends that emerge from these experiences are:

To me, this means that the conditions of my happiness are:

On the flip side of the coin of what's made us the happiest are the toughest battles we've ever had to face. As speakers, authors, and coaches, we believe that the most difficult adversities we face in life become catalysts to forge skills, principles, and wisdom that's meant for us. The examples are so prevalent that almost any massive success can attribute their drive, skills, and success to a formative event, person, or phase of their life that was far from enjoyable. Perhaps being bullied as a youth has made you into a stout advocate of justice. Maybe struggling in school has led you to buck the system and become a remarkable entrepreneur. We think you get the picture. Time to be brave and dive into the next exercise.

The toughest battle I've faced so far in my life is:

As a result, I want to ensure that I always:

Great work in going through the last exercise. It's tough self-work, and not everyone's up to the challenge. You're heading for great success on the simple fact that you were brave enough to do this work and turn it into meaning – well done!

Tying it together

Now that you've discovered the conditions of your success, and a form of what you're being beckoned to, let's assemble a purpose. What similarities emerged? Was there an opposite that formed? Let's imagine that Sarah was bullied, and justice is something she will always fight for.

Perhaps she feels compelled to seek injustice in different parts of the world and empower those less fortunate to join her on her personal improvement mission. She might start a charity, movement, or a business that leads hiking, kayaking, and other adventures in other parts of the world. She might invite affluent travelers to see areas of the world and social realities they otherwise never would.

Can you imagine how much she'd love to run a business that consistently introduced her to new people and new places, while she led amazing experiences for others? Can you imagine Sarah *ever* quitting that dream job?

We think you're getting the point of the exercise. Try thinking less of the job and more of the non-negotiables that truly matter to you. Try writing a statement like, "In my most important work it is imperative that I [am surrounded by, get to experience, receive/ give, achieve, etc.], while always [doing this, allowing that, condoning this, etc.]."

Another way of going about the Core Purpose is the oft-used, "If you had enough money that you never had to work again, how would you spend the rest of your life?"

Take some time, get in the right headspace for deeper work, and start thinking about your Core Purpose.

Now, that was a lot of deep, soul-searching hard work! Let's shift the focus back to the reason you bought this book – sales.

CHAPTER ONE
Pages Into Points

❖ Your Core Values underpin every major decision you make. We don't decide our Core Values, we discover them. Once uncovered, our values must be aligned with the work we are doing to be truly fulfilled. Values help us make should or should not decisions.

❖ Our Core Purpose guides our present to create a more ideal future. Our Core Purpose adds meaning to our work and our lives by answering the great 'why' questions, and even the simple 'why am I doing this?' ones.

Chapter Two

YOU are in sales!

"The language we use is extremely powerful. It is the frame through which we perceive and describe ourselves and our picture of the world."[6] *– Iben Dissing Sandahl*

According to Daniel Pink[7], in his book *To Sell Is Human*, one out of every nine Americans, and one in ten Canadians, works in a job that can be directly considered sales. Pink and his team pioneered an interesting study, "What Do You Do at Work?" wherein employees were asked to categorize their day into functional activities.[7] These activities were broken down into functional tasks and, through statistical analysis, the average North American professional spends 40% of their time in sales-like activities (persuading, engaging, and leading, etc.) that Pink calls "non-sales selling"[7]. Pink and his research team go on to conclude that while most professionals don't consider themselves in sales, on average we spend 24 minutes of every hour selling something in some way.[7]

In our collective experience, most professionals either classify themselves in a way that describes their expertise functionally; or they admit that they don't enjoy, feel confident, or skilled in sales. In other words, they reject embracing the act of selling in any way, by saying, "I'm a highly trained psychologist (doctor/personal trainer/lawyer/coach/accountant/massage therapist, etc.), I didn't go into this practice to sell." Or they mask fear, inexperience, or lack of skill in selling by claiming they are being more virtuous instead, "I don't want to feel like a slimy salesman."

If we consider Pink's research, two fifths of one's day is spent selling, convincing, and negotiating[7]; yet when it becomes formalized we succumb to fear, build up the sales process bigger than it needs to be, or we yield under our own negativity. This is not to say, "You're in sales anyway – get over it." The goal of this chapter is to reframe the sales process, and how we interpret our role in this process, so we can maximize value to the customer.

Put Yourself in Your Customers' Shoes

When was the last time you walked into an auto dealership when you knew, without a doubt, you did not want a new vehicle? Would you ever go to an appliance store when you had no need for a washer, dryer, or refrigerator? Of course not, why would you waste your valuable time?

If we accept these conclusions, it's not a far mental leap to conclude that your customers aren't going to waste their own time on purpose either. The first concept to embrace is that your customers came to you for a reason. _They have needs and you can potentially fulfill them_.

The next notion to remember is how customers behave. Well, how do you behave? Do you walk in with your credit card already out of your wallet, or do you ask questions? Of course, most customers ask questions. They want to know that the product or service they are vetting will meet their needs. To understand whether they've found the right solution for them, they will defer to the salesperson's knowledge. They will ask the questions, so the salesperson can recommend the right fit.

Fundamental to this assumption, is that the sales professional listens to, understands, and acts on behalf of their customers' best interests. In this sense, _every 'sleazy sales rep' that takes advantage of a customer's trust creates an opportunity for a well-intentioned, ethical sales professional like you_!

In short, your prospects are relying on you to understand their needs and recommend a solution that creates an ideal match. Your customers aren't walking into your business on guard – _they walk in hoping that you will help them buy!_

The last notion to remember if we are to reframe our view on what sales or selling feels like, is that you're a top-notch professional who knows their stuff! You're an asset to your customers and they may be lost without your direction. They may opt instead to blindly purchase a product that won't fit their needs, or they may be duped by someone less ethical than you who only sees a sales commission instead of a human being in front of them.

In short, _if you don't provide a valuable service to your customers, someone else is more than happy to take their money and offer them less value_.

In philosophy, argumentation theory proposes that if all the arguments in a given postulation are true, and the conclusion flows from the arguments, then the conclusion must be true.[8] In the context of this book, if you've agreed with the above, then you must accept their logical conclusion.

The arguments that almost everyone nods their heads to (in our experience) are;

1. Your customers have needs and you can potentially fulfill them. They came to you on purpose.

2. Your customers want and need you to help them buy.

3. By way of your experience and expertise, you can help your customers.

4. If you don't help your customers, they'll seek it elsewhere; often through vendors that'll provide lower quality products, services, advice, and experiences.

If we accept those arguments, then we're forced to consider, if not accept the notion, that _you have a moral duty to act in your customers' best interests and give them the best advice, service, and experience that you can_. If your offering is their solution, you have a moral obligation to provide that solution to them to the best of your abilities.

Is that a definition of "selling" that you can get behind?

Does that make you feel less sleazy and more professional to do what your customers need you to do?

Imagine you go to see a health and wellness professional. You tell them your goals are to lose 50 pounds, have more energy throughout the day, and you'd also like to address a nagging shoulder injury you've had for years. Would you feel like your needs are met if they sold you 3 personal training sessions? Would it feel like better service if they instead walked you through the process of rehabilitating your shoulder, and how that should start with an assessment with the teams' physiotherapist? If they suggested 3 physiotherapy sessions to address the shoulder, then said they would personally speak to the physiotherapist, and relay and shoulder-related information to your personal trainer, would you feel a lot more peace of mind?

In the above example – the proper solution for the client would cost more money, however saving money in this scenario doesn't solve your problem. The take home lesson here is to focus on providing the best service – not on making the sale.

The last notion to explore in this chapter is what kind of salesperson you are. If you've accepted that you're in sales and you can feel great about providing a service, now it's important to know what sort of sales environment you'd best thrive in. Of equal importance, it's critical for sales managers and business owners to build effective sales teams with different skills and natural tendencies.

For our purposes, there are three different types of sales professional: the hunter, the farmer, and the order taker. We will define each and explore their unique value to the sales organization.

The Hunter

The hunter is the quintessential outbound sales pro. They are, almost by rule, extroverted, confident, persistent, and thick-skinned. Whether by nature or nurture, they are used to hearing "no," then knocking on the next door or dialing the next number. To truly understand the psyche of a hunter, allow us to share an experience from our business coaching practice.

We were helping a client through the recruitment and selection of a new sales manager. Our client wanted to find a hunter who could one day be their Vice President of Business Development and Sales. The position they were looking to fill really called for a unicorn, and they found one. One of the candidates they did not select, however, perfectly typified a true hunter. In his exact words - in the interview - he said, "I really like autonomy. If I'm hitting my numbers, I'd like to be left alone. If I'm not hitting my numbers, fire me."

Every true hunter who just read that statement just nodded their head enthusiastically – didn't you?!

If your reaction to that statement was hesitation, perhaps even offense and detecting insubordination, then you may be a farmer. Before we define a farmer, let's make sure everyone understands the benefits and risks associated with a true hunter.

Hunter - the pros:

- prefers to be out selling than at their desk
- generates leads and sales out of seemingly nothing
- in most cases, does not require much management – just coaching from time to time
- competitive, achievement-oriented, and driven; and
- confident, builds rapport easily and quickly, often creates favorable first impressions on the company's behalf.

31

Hunter - the cons:

- rare
- most hunters defy convention, even rules – they're often rebels
- often motivated by money and can be lured by a better offer
- sometimes promise the world to their customers, only to have operations realize "we don't make that product" (or provide that service); and
- can be impatient; sometimes loses motivation for process work; that is, properly documenting paperwork or updating their Customer Relationship Management (CRM) database

The Farmer

The farmer, as the name may imply, is highly skilled at nurturing relationships over time. Farmers know that they must sow before they reap; they believe in, and practice, fostering long-term relationships. In a perfect world, with a budget large enough to hire both, the hunter closes the deal and goes back out to the hunting grounds, then the farmer steps in to make sure that the new customer is taken care of every step of the way.

A farmer is not a hand-holder; however, they genuinely care for their customers, and often end up becoming great, perhaps lifelong, friends with them.

The farmer is often great with names, remembering personal details, and going over and above. In one of our previous fitness businesses, we had a farmer who was so great with her busy executive personal training clients (who were often too busy to meal plan), that she made them lunches and brought them to their workplace!

Farmers are amazing with helping businesses improve their customer retention, which drives down the need for external marketing and lowers the average cost of client acquisition; and therefore, increases profit. In fact, retaining customers is six to seven times less expensive than acquiring new ones.[9] Farmers know what they're good at, but most do not feel entirely comfortable with hunting and farming. Farmers need to read, and reread the preceding section of this chapter, and they still may never feel comfortable in a true outbound sales environment. They're usually outside their comfort zone (and often, outside their skill set), and sometimes feel sleazy in true outbound sales scenarios. This is the part of the chapter where you true farmers are nodding your heads in agreement!

Farmer - the pros:

- great at creating and nurturing lasting relationships
- often able to recover frustrated or even departed customers
- helps improve customer retention and lower marketing and client acquisition costs
- better at following systems and playing by the rules than hunters

- when treated well and compensated fairly, farmers enjoy long careers with the same organization. They're loyal, which saves money on rehiring and retraining new team members; and
- often help generate referrals by keeping existing customers happy. Many farmers are more comfortable asking a friend for a referral than they are asking a stranger for a sale.

Farmer - the cons:

- very rare to find a hybrid hunter/farmer; farmers generally (though not always) close fewer sales
- depending on your specific business, it may take a long time to prove return on investment (ROI) for a farmer's compensation
- farmers who run their own businesses generally face some very lean years during the start-up phase. Many of their good businesses will fail if they can't learn to hunt confidently and authentically; and
- farmers may sometimes become 'too close' to their customers, and customer retention efforts turn into social hangouts.

The Order Taker

The order taker is the third kind of salesperson. By order taker, most sales academics and professionals refer to a reactive approach to sales. Instead of cold calling, networking, or other means of generating new business, order takers typically work in inbound sales and take the orders of customers who are already somewhat interested and likely to buy.

Order takers are often comfortable in conversation once the ball gets rolling; however, like most farmers they are usually not comfortable in pure prospecting scenarios. Order takers are generally much better at following systems and accurately filling out paperwork and sales contracts than hunters (and many farmers, for that matter).

If an organization does not invest in marketing, the true value of an order taker goes unrealized. In other words, it's hard to justify their salary if no leads are coming through the door looking to buy.

The great news for order takers is that many of the skills that make hunters or farmers great can be learned. This means that instead of worrying about the company's budget and the justification for their position, they can learn how to add more value. An order taker may learn how to network more effectively and to prospect, or cultivate new sales through existing clients, for example. When they can do this, order takers often have the advantage against their hunter or farmer peers of being more thorough and methodical in their approach (and most sales leaders love a team member who is spot on with their paperwork and diligent with their CRM)!

Order Taker - the pros:

- often very detailed; their paperwork gets sent back less than most hunters
- trainable from a systems perspective; and

- more introverted than most hunters, order takers cause fewer workplace conflicts than many hunters who can be far more direct and to the point.

Order Taker - the cons:

- need to be coached, trained, and inspired to be more proactive around selling and prospecting or it becomes hard to calculate return on investment (ROI) on their salary. Thus, they often become the first to go in a down quarter or year
- can sometimes become too methodical; struggling with the notion of letting a sales conversation flow more naturally; and
- a salesperson who is naturally an order taker, hired by a small company to be their one sales professional, will likely struggle with the amount of prospecting and selling that their role (and budget) dictates.

It's important to note that any skill a hunter, farmer, or order taker has that makes them great can be learned. Any sales professional can diversify their skills to add more value to their organization or business. It's also critical for their success that any sales professional seek out the kinds of environments in which they are most likely to flourish. How to set oneself up for success is exactly where we begin the next chapter.

CHAPTER TWO
Pages Into Points

- ❖ Your customers have needs, and you are in a position to help them as a result of your training, experience, skills, and genuine care.
- ❖ As a result of the above, you have a moral obligation to help your customers to the best of your abilities, or somebody else is happy to just take their money.
- ❖ Not all salespeople are created equal. Rather than trying to fit a square peg into a round hole, read up on the three types of salesperson and find out which type you are most likely to enjoy and flourish as.

Chapter Three

Set yourself up for success

"Success is where preparation and opportunity meet." - Bobby Unser

Long before your prospect makes a purchase decision, they have a gut feeling about you and your offering. This gut feeling is a reaction to your presentation, your marketing, your approach, your people skills, and how **well you've done your job**. Because we're advocating a consultative and interactive methodology of client acquisition, a mission-critical part of your job is to know your client. More important than your product or industry knowledge is how well you know your *customer*. As a side note, we use client and customer interchangeably; though typically we define customer in a product sales environment, and client in a service business environment. In other words, book stores have customers, while financial advisors have clients.

A client (or prospect) who doesn't feel listened to, heard or cared for, is only going to care so much about how well you know your own business. A prospect who is having a tremendous experience and feels that they've just made a new friend, however, wants to buy from you. This does not in any way mean that we're advocating cutting corners and skipping your research; rather, it's a reminder to prioritize your client and your business.

We recommend sales professionals and business owners consider their homework in two distinct phases;

1. tactical research on your prospect
2. self-preparedness and showing up as the best version of yourself

Tactical Research

The more you know before a sales meeting about who you're selling to, the easier the conversation flows and the more it seems like you know the answer to all their questions. Most of the time it's because you DO know the answer to their questions because you're able to forecast the kind of questions they'll likely ask.

'Wouldn't it take a mind reader to know what questions they're going to ask?' you're likely asking yourself, and you're right. In using our approach, you can become a mind reader of sorts because you know what your client is going to be thinking!

You will know what your client is likely thinking because you've considered why they're coming to you in the first place, what problems they have, what matters to them, and what they really want and need.

When going into a sales meeting with a prospect, your homework checklist should be as follows (not all will be applicable to you depending on your role, industry, or buyer profile of course);

Business to Consumer (B2C) Sales

- Where do they work? Where do they live? Does your location matter in the purchase decision, and, if so, how can you overcome any distance or inconvenience objections before they come up?
- Depending on the industry they work in, are you booking a meeting that's convenient for your customer where they'll be engaged and relaxed? Try not to book a prospect on their Monday. For example, for those working in restaurants and bars, Tuesday is often their Monday, so a Thursday meeting might be best.
- What stage of life are they in? Are you trying to sell life insurance to a high school grad, or income protection to a retiree? You need to anticipate and know your customers' needs, goals, and challenges as they transition through different stages of life.
- Have they done business with your firm in the past? What did they buy? Who did they buy from? What kind of intel can you uncover by going through your company's systems, documentation, and speaking to your teammates?
- What are their lifestyle factors that will influence or affect their purchase decision?
- Are they the primary decision maker? Do they need to consult their spouse, their family, or a business partner before committing to buy?
- Do you have a mutual colleague, friend, or client who can give you more background information on your prospect?

- The million-dollar question: WHY are they buying or considering buying? A married man might purchase a second property because he and his family are considering an investment property, or he might be going through a divorce. How you talk to this buyer would change dramatically if you knew their backstory and why they're considering buying.

Business to Business (B2B) Sales

- Check the company website
  - How long have they been in business?
  - Who's their ideal client or customer? Is this obvious from their website?
  - Company history/ about us section: what are their Core Values? What is their company history? Who are the founders? What's the story of the company?
- Check out their corporate social media profile(s). What insights can you glean from reviewing their Facebook, Twitter, Instagram, and other feeds?
- Know exactly where they are located if the company has a brick and mortar location. Know exactly where you will park, and how long the commute will take from wherever your previous appointment, your office, or home is.
- How well do you know their industry?

- What do you think their pain points would be?
- What might the major opportunities be?
- What technological advancements or potential disruptive innovations are headed into their industry that they should be preparing for?

Everyone is busy. As business owners ourselves we receive a lot of pitches every day. One way to blow the sale right away is to forget or forgo your research. If a seller has not checked out our company, what we do, and why we may or may not need their services, it becomes way too easy to say "no!"

In addition to researching your prospects, there are six professional traits that help set a salesperson up for success and endear them to their customers.

Empathy

When talking to a potential client, it's very important that you get on the same page as them and take the time to genuinely understand where they're coming from. Have you ever had a conversation with someone and they just don't get it? Bad salespeople don't really take the time to find out what the problems are; and thus, they either don't make the sale, or the customer later regrets the purchase.

By being empathetic to a prospect's situation, you'll be better able to provide them with a solution that will HELP them versus merely selling them something to try and hit your target.

Focused

It doesn't matter how empathetic you are as a salesperson, if you can't stay focused, you're not going to get anywhere. As a successful salesperson (which you are going to be), it's very important that you're self-motivated and able to hold yourself to a high standard, and focused on your top priorities.

Furthermore, we coach a lot of sales professionals who struggle with their confidence in the sales meeting, particularly when it comes time to present their offer. Our number one tip for remaining confident and presenting the best version of yourself and your business – is to focus on your customer, not yourself or how you are coming across. Furthermore, as the conversation drifts towards price, we always recommend keeping the focus on value (what the customer receives) instead of price (what they pay).

Persistent

An extension of focus, the ability to stay with tasks is essential. This becomes more challenging when those tasks are selling a product or service and we hear "no" or nothing at all. The truly remarkable sales professionals we've worked with can persist despite setbacks, and regardless of the inevitable emotional highs and lows. Their persistence leads directly to more input (as in – more prospecting reach outs). All other variables being held constant, a more persistent salesperson will make more prospecting attempts, and through that alone will win more contracts. Persistence pays!

Responsible

If you're going to succeed in sales, then you need to take responsibility for when something doesn't go according to plan. Sometimes your manager or client might want to share some advice or feedback with you. Try not to get defensive and start blaming it on other people, circumstances, market forces or anything else.

To move forward, you may need to take a step back to reassess the situation. By doing this, you'll be able to see what works and what doesn't – and take a corrective course of action that nets a positive benefit for all parties.

Positive

It's been said that "you never get a second chance to make a first impression," and it's true. The first chapter described "win-win selling" as relationship-based. How many relationships have you started when you were in a fit of rage; or muttering around with a figurative dark cloud over your head? The more positive and optimistic an attitude you embrace, the more you're able to spread this to others. People want to buy from people they like.

Furthermore, the more elevated our mood, the more optimistic we tend to be about what opportunities are available to us. This could affect the options you present a prospect in a sales meeting, or it could affect your entire sales strategy!

We like to take a positive disposition and impose certainty of positive outcomes. Basically, we suggest *deciding* that things are going to go your way. In other words, step one would be to embrace "I'm going to look for the positive in every situation today," and step two would then be "I'm positive I am going to get the sale in my next meeting".

Embrace a positive attitude and envision nothing but positive outcomes in all that you do. Your mind is a powerful tool – watch what it can unleash by bringing more positivity into your life and in the lives of others!

Social

The most common trait linking highly effective sales professionals we have encountered is their social orientation. Great sales people love people. Now there are some recluses out there who love technology (or products or whatever it is that they sell) who genuinely dislike people who may still make decent sales people. The great ones, however, are motivated by solving their customers' challenges and forming great relationships along the way.

Extreme introverts dread networking events, while highly social salespeople can attend three such events in a week and not feel like they're working at all. After all, isn't a networking event just a party with friends you haven't met yet?

When your research is complete, you're now able to show up prepared for the meeting – but are you emotionally prepared? In his famous study on verbal and nonverbal communication, Albert Mehrabian[10] discovered that only 7% of what we communicate is based on the actual words we use (verbal communication), 55% of what we communicate comes across from body language, and 38% via our paralanguage (the inflections, pauses, and other variations in the volume, tone, and delivery of our voice).

While this isn't a book on behavioral psychology, it's important to understand the consequences of not only what we're saying, but *also how we're saying it*. Imagine buying a new shirt. The salesperson says, "This shirt would look great on you at your next networking event." Now read that same sentence with the emphasis shifting each time and notice how you imagine the words being spoken.

A.   "THIS shirt would look great on you at your next networking event."

B.   "This shirt would look greeaaat on you at your next networking event."

C.   "This shirt would look great on YOU at your next networking event."

So how did you hear those sentences? Most people we tested this sentence on heard this;

A.   The focus was on the shirt - THIS is THE shirt - why bother looking at any other shirt?

B.   Sarcasm: the salesperson is making fun of me, what a jerk!

C.   Me. The salesperson is talking to me - they are focusing on me and only me.

Not one word changed, nor did the order change, and the same person we asked heard three different things when they heard the exact same sentence three times in a row. Even after a simple exercise like this, it becomes clear how important it is to show up to every meeting not only rehearsed, but *ready to deliver!*

So how do we show up ready to communicate exactly what we want to, in exactly the way our prospect wants to hear us? Time to learn how to control, change, and optimize your mental and emotional states.

State

Considering the gravity of Mehrabian's research, it becomes imperative to understand our body language and paralanguage and control the subliminal and nonverbal messages we are sending to our prospects.

Wood, Quinn, and Kashy[11] discuss how in non-habitual situations (any daily occurrence that hasn't been programmed into subconscious patterns through repetition), our thoughts are the precursor to our emotions, which are the precursor to our actions.

Our stance is that if we want different results, the only way to get there is through different actions. Reverse engineering the human path to action considering Wood et al.'s research, we can conclude that different results stem from changing our thoughts.

If we want to engage our potential clients in a captivating conversation that leads to the formation of a trusted advisor relationship that lasts years, it would go a long way to show up;

- genuinely interested in our prospect
- in a relaxed, yet professional manner

- prepared, researched, yet not too rehearsed so that our homework can come up in a conversation-friendly tone
- alert, aware, but not overpowering or intimidating
- smiling, listening, and understanding what your prospect is saying (and asking)

Most professionals will wear a suit and tie, shine their shoes, and make sure their hair (and makeup as the case may dictate) is spot on. With no attention to our inner make-up, however, we may well be walking into a meeting wholly unprepared.

If thought dictates emotion, and emotion dictates action[8], then the place to start to consistently choosing better actions is to choose better thoughts. This may be a revolutionary notion for many, but, yes, you can choose your thoughts!

This is not to say that negative, unwanted, or distracting thoughts come into your mind by choice. These things can happen because our mind wanders. According to Dr. Joseph Murray[12], our conscious mind has power over our subconscious mind to choose our thoughts, replace thoughts we aren't happy with, and to accept as true or dismiss as false impressions we get from the outside world.

If our beliefs and thoughts dictate our emotions, which dictate our actions, and the above can be chosen, then Wood et al. and Dr. Murray's work can help us conclude that we can choose, and change, our mental hardwiring.[11,12] We can choose to operate at a higher level!

Critical to the foundation of this mental model is the ability to filter out negative thoughts, rejection, and harmful messages from others. According to Dr. Murray, "A suggestion cannot impose itself on the subconscious mind against the will of the conscious mind." [12] We have "the power to reject the suggestion" as Dr. Murray puts it. [12] Furthermore, he notes that suggestions have no power until we accept them mentally and we can change the assumptions or beliefs from our subconscious if we become aware of the assumptions or beliefs that we are operating from. [12]

For example, a salesperson who thinks that he is a 'poor closer' may tell himself that he is a more natural farmer who's a nurturer of existing clients, than a hunter who is an acquirer of new leads and customers. He may find joy in this work, but he'll never know if he could be a great hunter unless he dispels the limiting belief that he is a poor closer and replaces it with a thought that he can accept as true. He may not be able to go from 'I'm a poor closer' to 'I'm the world's greatest closer,' but he may be able to replace the negative belief with 'I create trust in buyers right away because I am genuine, caring, and knowledgeable.' Could he become a great hunter or closer with this attitude? Of course!

Dr. Murray's work is so instrumental to mental and emotional preparedness, and optimizing our internal state, that we want to highlight two more notions of his research. First, replacing a negative or limiting belief with a positive or helpful belief may be challenging for some. Dr. Murray suggests many techniques to help this process, including visualizing the results you want to achieve, prayer, positive affirmations, and mantras repeated daily to hardwire the new thought or belief at the subconscious level.[12]

Second, Dr. Murray suggests a three-step process to success. Simply,

1. "Find the thing you love to do, then do it."[12] How can one possibly be a success if they don't love, or at least thoroughly enjoy, what they do?
2. Specialize or find your niche within your industry or calling.[12] This might be specializing in heavy machinery sales, or it might be specializing through your selling techniques. If most professionals hate cold calling, you might find a way to love cold calling and this might be the key to your success.
3. Your work cannot be wholly selfish – it must help you and others.[12] This is a profound truth, and one that helps us feel less 'salesy' as Daniel Pink describes how so many people view salespeople[7].

Especially considering the third step (which Murray describes as the most important step[12]), this philosophy enables sales professionals who don't consider themselves as sharks or natural closers to find their path to sales success. It is the backbone of the helping-customers-buy philosophy, which allows us to shift from trying to get customers to part with their wallets to providing a valuable, helpful service. Who can't feel great about providing a valuable, helpful service for others?

Our physical state

Now that we have examined our mental and emotional state, it's important to address our physical state, so we can master the 55% of communication accounted for through body language.[10]

When we can understand and manipulate the variables within our control, we show up as the best version of ourselves. Here are just a few examples of what your body language may be communicating;

- Arms crossed often means closed off – be it to new ideas, a negotiation, or the sale
- Leaning back may mean disinterested, or it may even mean intimidated
- Leaning forward conveys interest and engagement, even confidence
- Nodding one's head (as in yes), or sideways with a raised eyebrow often denotes agreement, interest, or even intrigue
- Shifting weight from one hip to the other when standing, tapping feet (sitting or standing), shifting gaze or looking at one's watch all signify someone is growing impatient
- Rolling eyes, frowning, drawing the head aback, or a stifled gasp all point to disagreement or even disdain; and
- A smile is often said to be authentic only when crow's feet form (smile lines) at the corners of the eyes.

So, we know WHY this is important, now HOW do we take control of our bodies to communicate what we want?

The first step is to decide how we want to show up. For most selling scenarios, the seller wants to convey confidence, knowledge, attentiveness, and genuine interest in the potential buyer. A salesperson who is so nervous they can barely remember their name won't be able to focus on building rapport with their prospective customer, right?

According to renowned performance coach and sport psychologist Dr. Peter Jensen, athletes can turn pressure into performance, yet professionals often describe pressure as stress or feeling overwhelmed.[13] By being able to tap into the nervous energy that goes into a game day situation, we can turn nervous energy into peak state performance energy.

Physically, the below-noted states have physical behaviors that are typical. Table 3.1 below gives a high-level overview of desired states and physical typifiers.

Table 3.1: Emotional States and Associated Behaviors

Desired State	Associated Physical Behavior
Confidence	Head up, proud chest, forward posture in conversation, able to maintain eye contact, firm handshake, shoulders back, commanding presence and gait

Knowledge-able	Relaxed (one who does not know their material will be hyper-focused on every word to formulate a response that makes them sound knowledgeable), head nodding vertically or sideways while listening (a sign of curiosity and engaged listening), may also show up like signs of confidence
Attentive	Eyes open, eyebrows often raising, head nodding in agreement or to one side as a sign of curiosity, open palms, arms not crossed or folded, leaning forward, may rest chin on hand (thinker pose), frequent and sustained eye contact
Genuine Interest	Very similar to attentive, though genuine interest conveys more signs of emotion; more smiles (especially with the eyes - look for the crow's feet'), more laughs as well as more questions - especially questions that aren't self-serving (for example, "Tell me more" or "How does that work?" instead of "Can I show you more about our offering?"

Far more effective, however, than memorizing physical traits from a list and trying to mimic postures is embracing the above-noted states (or whichever ones you desire) psychologically. For instance, rather than feigning interest to close the sale, your body language will adjust itself. Furthermore, work by Boundless[3] describes this sort of approach as relationship selling and concludes that this approach is predicated upon "authenticity, genuine concern, and honesty. It's not a sales technique that can be simulated without possessing [these] qualities."[3]

In short, being genuinely interested in your customer and being aware of how you're showing up – and how you WANT to show up – are the keys to win-win selling success.

```
┌─────────────────────────────────────────┐
│          CHAPTER THREE                    │
│         Pages Into Points                 │
│                                           │
│  ❖ Preparation is critical to success. Your │
│     tactical research prior to each and every │
│     sales meeting cannot be skipped or    │
│     skimmed.                              │
│  ❖ As - if not more important than your   │
│     homework – is your self work. The     │
│     physical and emotional state you bring │
│     to each meeting has profound effects on │
│     how each meeting goes.                │
└─────────────────────────────────────────┘
```

CHAPTER THREE
Pages Into Points

- ❖ Preparation is critical to success. Your tactical research prior to each and every sales meeting cannot be skipped or skimmed.
- ❖ As - if not more important than your homework – is your self work. The physical and emotional state you bring to each meeting has profound effects on how each meeting goes.

PART TWO

KNOW YOUR CUSTOMER

Chapter Four

Know your customer

"Nobody cares how much you know until they know how much you care"   *- Theodore Roosevelt*

As chapter two concluded, when you truly care about your customer, you feel great about helping them buy. We can't truly care about our customer unless we are willing to get to know them. Very, very well.

This chapter is designed to get you to think of exactly who your perfect customer is for your product or service offering. Try to be as specific as possible and watch the ideal customer come to life right in front of your eyes. Ours is a very thorough, perhaps exhaustive checklist. While not every question below will relate to your ideal customer, and while the questions will change if you're in B2B versus B2C sales, the point is to cover your bases and build a robust description that helps focus your sales and marketing efforts. Answer all the areas that apply and disregard those that are not applicable to your customers. We acknowledge that this will be a lot of work up front, but it'll pay dividends on the backend – we promise. Have fun with this exercise!

For the purposes of this exercise we will name our ideal customers Jack and Miranda Thomas. Giving your ideal customer avatar a name, and as detailed a backstory as possible, adds an emotional connection. This will anchor your sales strategy, marketing initiatives, and how you brand and describe your offering. See our example below.

Customer Avatar Worksheet

Name(s)

- Jack and Miranda Thomas

Age

- Jack is 53
- Miranda is 49

Physical Appearance

Height

- Jack is 6'1"
- Miranda is 5'6"

Weight

- Jack is approximately 190 pounds
- a gentleman would never ask! However, to help create a mental picture, Miranda is 130 pounds

Build

- Athletic, great posture, lean with decent musculature
- Healthy but not athletic like Jack

Other defining physical characteristics

- Jack has mostly grey hair, short and clean cut. He has a smooth goatee that is almost entirely white, and a you-won't-forget-it firm handshake. Jack normally dresses business casual, sometimes in jeans, and when he and Miranda head out on date night, it's a three-piece suit or sport coat and dress slacks over a great shirt (no tie) and the top button undone.

- Miranda has green eyes. Her long brown hair sometimes features blonde highlights. Perhaps her most memorable trait is her laugh.

Background

Country of origin if different from current country of residence: Jack was raised outside of Grand Rapids, Minnesota; and Miranda hails from just outside of Portland, Oregon originally. They met through mutual friends after both having eventually relocated to Denver, Colorado.

- How long have they been in this country? Since birth
- Why did they move to this country? N/A
- What do they miss about their original country? N/A
- What do they love about their new country of choice? N/A

Intellectual

Education level (High school / College/ University Degree/ Masters/etc.)

- Jack has an MBA from Stanford
- Miranda has a Master's Degree in education from Oregon State

Personal development

- What news channel do they watch? Jack – BNN; Miranda – BBC
- What books are trending for them? Jack – *Good to Great* by Jim Collins; Miranda – *Believe in the Possibility* by Michelle Obama
- What magazines do they read: Jack – Success, Forbes, ESPN NFL draft and fantasy football preview issues; Miranda – Wine Enthusiast, US Weekly, Shape magazine
- What newspapers do they read: Jack – NY Times; Miranda - none

Career

What industry do they work in? (examples: information technology, finance, research, agriculture, construction, energy, biomedical, etc.)

- Jack: oil and gas
- Miranda: education

What positions do they hold? (for example: Entry level/ Mid-level/ Management/ Director/ Owner/ Board of Directors/ Volunteer)

- Jack: Regional director of business development, western US
- Miranda: Internal staff curriculum resource (advisor to teachers)

Household Income

- Jack's income per year? $275,000 USD

- Miranda's income per year? $68,000 USD

What is the household combined income? $343,000 USD

How many people contribute to this household income (i.e. family members): 2

Investments

- What does your ideal client avatar's retirement plan look like? Jack and Miranda's combined retirement savings (including their 401K and mutual funds) just eclipsed $1M USD. Their goal is to retire with over $3M.
- Are your ideal clients in a position to weather an unexpected financial crisis? Jack and Miranda could live comfortably for 3 months without touching their retirement savings.

Family Residence

- Where do they live? Jack and Miranda live in Golden, Colorado; a quaint suburb west of Denver that allows them the amenities of a first-class city, as well as a quick escape to the mountains and a more relaxed pace of living.
- Value of home? Their 2900 sq. ft. home on 15th street is valued at $796,000 USD
- Where is all the furniture purchased? Most of their furniture was purchased from Element home furniture
- Who assists with the design of the house? One of Miranda's best friends is an interior designer by trade. She and Miranda discuss

interior design and decorating ideas regularly over wine.

Second home

- Where is the location? Jack and Miranda are looking for a place in Mexico's Mayan Riviera
- How far is this location? A four-hour flight to Cancun, then a one-hour drive to the community they are looking to purchase in
- What is the purpose of this second home? (Relax/ Skiing/ Business, etc.) Their second home will be a beach relaxation and family vacation spot for hosting their friends and extended family

Family

- How many children? Jack and Miranda have three teenage children
- How old are the children? Raelyn, their eldest, is 17; Ethan is 15; and Cole is 14.
- School of choice for the children? Cole attends the local sport private school; while Raelyn attends the nearest Catholic High School, and Cole attends middle school that he begged his parents to let him attend based on the strength of their baseball team.
- Children's regular activities, dance, hockey, etc.? Raelyn has a part-time job at a fashion retailer at the local mall and is very focused on her studies as she hopes to get into a great school for University. Ethan is all about hockey and plans to play NCAA or semi-pro after high school. Cole plays baseball and is also quite the budding artist. He draws his

own comic books, complete with superheroes he created. The entire family also enjoys the terrific skiing Colorado offers.

Cars

What car(s) do they drive?

- Jack drives an Infinity QX 50 sport utility vehicle; while Miranda drives an Audi Q7. They both prefer an SUV that is good on winter roads and can haul the kids' sports equipment or take the family skiing. Jack and Miranda tend to get a new vehicle every five to ten years, though it was more frequent when their family was growing. Given that they both drive higher-end vehicles, Jack and Miranda generally only get their vehicles serviced at the dealership that they bought their SUVs from.

Recreational crafts and vehicles

Do they have a boat, motorbike, off-road vehicles, etc.?

- Jack and his sons all have all-terrain vehicles that they enjoy in Colorado's rural areas through the trails in the spring and summer. Jack also has a snowmobile for the winter. The family considers a boat every spring, but they don't get to the lake often enough and their best friends have a boat they use regularly.

Health, Fitness & Beauty

What do they do to look and feel their best?

- Jack would rather hike, fish, canoe, or spend time outdoors than hit the gym. However, he does keep a membership at a fitness and racquet club nearby where he sometimes plays squash with business associates or the kids and goes for the odd swim and sauna. He runs sporadically in the warmer months but would never describe himself as a runner.
- Miranda is a member of the same club and plays squash in the winter and tennis outside in the summer. She also works with a personal trainer one to two times a week when work, travel, and the kids' schedules permit.

Social

What clubs are they a member of?

- Jack is a member of a petroleum association, as well as a business peer forum. Miranda was part of a local parent volunteer group but has had to take a hiatus in the past few years as commuting due to the kids' activities has ramped up.

What sports do they support?

- The family all cheer for the Denver Broncos and Colorado Avalanche hockey team; however, due to his Minnesota roots, Jack still has a soft spot for the Minnesota Vikings.

- Entertaining and going out

63

- Jack and Miranda love to host and have the perfect house to do so. They have a dinner party or larger get together almost every month. They also have a few restaurants they enjoy, from Boston Pizza after one of the kids' games to a steak and seafood lounge perfect for a couple's night out. They eat out about once a week either as a family or as a couple, but most meals are cooked at home. Whenever possible they try to eat in the dining room as a family, with no television on or electronics at the table.

What other pastime activities do they have?

- Besides the kids' activities, occasionally eating out, and the odd Broncos or Avalanche game, the Thomas family goes out to movies approximately once every two months. They'll also take in two or three concerts a year, but usually not as a whole family as they can't agree on music! Jack loves country and classic rock; while Miranda loves 80's music, and the kids are a mix of hard rock, techno, and (according to Jack), "God knows what that is."

Legacy

What Non-profit organizations do they support?

- Jack and Miranda are regular supporters of Parkinson's research because Miranda lost her dad to Parkinson's five years ago. They also, by way of their kids' activities, end up supporting youth sports activities quite often.

Are they on the board of directors for the non-profit(s) they support?

- Not at present, though Miranda has thought about joining the Parkinson's board as a director at large when the chauffeuring years as a parent slow down.

Are they part of the fundraising or organizing committees?

- Not currently

How do they relax and unwind?

- Miranda enjoys yoga and, although inconsistent, she also enjoys her Headspace meditation app. As noted previously, Miranda also works with a personal trainer and enjoys time outdoors with the family, be it skiing or camping.
- Jack prefers to spend his time outdoors and doing activities with the kids. Nothing beats a Vikings game with the kids for him, whether when they come to Denver or when the family returns home to Minnesota.

Travel

Where, how often, and for how long do they travel?

- Jack and Miranda take a few trips back to Minnesota to visit Jack's family each year. They also like to take several ski weekends since they're so close to the Colorado mountains. With Denver being such a hub for major airlines, the Thomas family has many options in terms of their annual beach vacation! They generally alternate between Hawai'i, Mexico, or a Caribbean holiday; though, once every five years or so, they may forgo the beach for Europe, or do both as they did two years ago during their trip to Spain and the south of France.

Personality

- How would you describe their personalities? This may or may not be useful for your ideal avatar, but in a B2B setting, many professionals have used a personality profiling tool such as DISC, SDI, Meyers-Briggs, or True Colors
- Using language impartial to any of the above profiling tools, Jack is an assertive, confident, vocal leader. He's not afraid to take charge, though he is also respectful and wants to hear from everyone in the room before making big decisions. He has thick skin when it comes to conflict, hardened by all the "no's" one hears after decades working in business development.
- Miranda seems to have a sixth sense. When people really want to know how a meeting went, or how others felt after an important decision or conflict, they turn to Miranda. She always seems to have everyone's best interests at heart, fiercely loyal, and a bit of a mother bear when it comes to her family.

A day in the life of

- What does an average week day look like for Jack?
  - Wake up time: 5:30am
  - Tasks / duties before leaving the house: workout, shower, shave (does this at home or at the club), initial email check, review to do list
  - Commute time to work: it depends – the commute to the office is 20 minutes. If visiting a potential customer, the commute could be over an hour if on the other side of Denver, or several hours if by plane.
  - Work (home) timetable: Jack can be sending emails by 6:00 a.m. and might close his laptop by 11:00 p.m. if he's in the middle of an important deal or year-end preparation.
  - Lunch partner; that is, eating out / eating at home (office) / eating with who: Jack tries to maximize his time by booking meetings almost every lunch hour. Every now and then he makes a priority to lunch with his wife or kids (if they're not in school).
  - Commute time home from work: as above, varies.
  - After work activities: family time, also more work in the form of email catch up. Dinner as a family then either watching TV, unwinding with a beer or glass of wine, or walking the dog.
  - Bedtime: most nights by 10:00 p.m.
- What does an average week day look like for Miranda?

- Wake up time: 6:45 a.m.
- Tasks / duties before leaving the house: kids' lunches, making sure the kids have everything they need, and they get to school on time.
- Commute time to work: 15 minutes
- Work (home) timetable: home by 4:00 p.m.
- Lunch partner; that is, eating out / eating at home (office) / eating with who: coworkers
- Commute time home from work: 20 minutes
- After work activities: more work happens after hours depending on seasonal and short-term needs.
- Bedtime: most nights by 10:00 p.m.
- What does an average weekend look like?
  - Wake up time: Jack and Miranda generally sleep in until 7:30 a.m.; although, Jack is often up earlier
  - Activities: physical activity, kids' sports or activities, skiing or a Broncos or Avalanche game
  - Bedtime: between 11:00 p.m. and 1:00 a.m.

Additional comments to help understand your ideal customer avatar more clearly.

Anything else you can think of here that allows you to clearly picture your ideal customer, and to help you understand them - if not think like them. The better you understand your avatar - even if hypothetical when you first start a new job or launch a new business - allows you to understand how they like to make their purchase decisions, which allows you to understand how, where, and when to approach them as a sales professional.

If you don't know at first, guess. As your business (or career) grows, you will either validate your guesswork as true, or you'll adjust and clarify your avatar through experience and customer data.

Putting your avatar into practice

Let's say you sell sporting goods, and you specialize in high-end golf gear and attire. Your ideal avatar might be the resident professionals at high-end golf and country clubs. If your market was the Pacific Northwest, specializing in Seattle, you might have done research to know that three of the top five professionals live in Bellevue, Washington (hypothetical example). Further research may lead you to know that they all stop by the same boutique coffee shop on their way to their different clubs, and two of them share the same personal trainer. Furthermore, you might uncover that they all refer their clients to the same wealth advisory firm.

This information becomes extremely powerful in two ways;

1. You could frequent the same coffee shop, and try a few workouts with their personal trainer, in hopes of meeting your golf professionals directly, or being referred to them.
2. The wealth advisory firm could become an invaluable strategic partnership. Perhaps you

can take some of the top advisors out for a few rounds of golf or invite their firm to be a sponsor for an upcoming tournament. They're sure to receive free or discounted green fees or swag, and you share a client base. Golfers tend to be affluent, so the advisory firm and you as the sales professional might both be targeting the golf pros, and yet in no way acting as competition for one another. The firm might, in fact, open their network to you which would open many new leads and opportunities (and you could do the same for them).

It's important to note that client privacy and non-disclosure must not be compromised. We're not suggesting sharing proprietary information, client lists, or any other unprofessional or unethical behavior. Rather, this approach leads to many more warm introductions, which lead to much more likely sales.

Now that you have a much greater understanding of who you are in the business of helping, let's shift our attention to your customers and how they want to buy.

CHAPTER FOUR
Pages Into Points

- ❖ The most successful companies and salespeople get to know their target market better than that market knows themselves.
- ❖ Creating a highly detailed and specific client avatar should include demographic, and most importantly, psychographic typifiers to help you understand and serve your ideal target market.
- ❖ Once you know exactly who you are selling to, you can create a more strategic sales and marketing plan, including forming strategic partnerships with non-competitive businesses who already serve your customers.

Chapter Five

Know how your customers want to buy!

Fundamental to the notion that this book will help you *sell in any economy* is that we have done our share of market research on how customers want to buy. How can anyone propose to sell in any economy unless they've considered almost every type of customer and their buying motivation?

We want to answer this question. Our approach is simple. We asked thousands of consumers in Canada and the United States one simple question. Our 100% anonymous, one-question survey asked, *"When dealing with a sales person, the way I like to be treated as a customer, and the way I like to make my purchase decisions, is as follows…"*

Of the answers we received, 32 distinct, though related, trends emerged. The top ten we received are shown in Table 5.1 below. They paint a very clear picture on how consumers want to buy!

Table 5.1: Summary of Sales Survey Responses

	Top Trends	%
1	Understand my needs	10.98%
2	Listen before suggesting	8.54%
3	Educate me	7.01%
4	Be knowledgeable	6.71%
5	Focus on my best interests	6.10%
6	Treat me with respect	5.79%
7	Low/ no pressure approach	5.18%
8	Be helpful	5.18%
9	Know your value proposition - how are you better?	4.57%
10	Be available, but not hovering	4.27%

The top responses can be simplified into a singular piece of advice. If we were to do that, the countless pages of responses can be reduced to two sentences: *"Don't just sell me whatever it is you're being paid to sell me. Take the time to understand my needs before making suggestions on what you think would be ideal for me."*

To this point we've advocated a customer-centric approach. Customers from Northern Alberta to Southern Florida are singing the same song. There were several other key phrases in our survey that support this approach as well, such as "Be genuine/authentic" in 11th place with 3.96% of responses, "Let me lead/ ask questions" in 12th, "Give me options" in 14th, "Give me time" in 15th, "Ask me questions" in 16th, and "Cater your approach" in 19th.

It's important to note that more than 10% of all respondents mentioned a low-pressure approach. More than 5% used those words exactly, while 4.27% mentioned "Be available, but not hovering," and 3.66% selected "Let me lead," while another 3.05% pleaded, "Give me time."

While there's more wisdom to glean by reviewing all 32 trends (see Appendix A at the back of this book), the take home message is quite simple: it's all about the customer.

A great sales professional will seek to understand the customer's agenda rather than enforcing their own.

A desperate salesperson will come across as pushy; while a true professional will give a customer time and add value in every interaction.

In an article for the National Association of Sales Professionals, Alen Mayer recommends listening as the key to success[14] – even when cold calling. He recommends a loose script, including your main points and your most likely objections (with how to overcome), especially for introverts. However, he lists the function of truly listening to your potential customer as the real key to cold calling success.[14]

The kind of salesperson who leaves customers with buyer's remorse, or a bad taste in their mouths, sees potential buyers as walking commissions; while a true sales rock star sees a person that they genuinely care about and want to help.

If the first two chapters seemed like a fairy tale. Perhaps you thought, 'I can't imagine selling and not feeling icky', then let the data trends from across

North America prove to you that honest, professional, helpful salespeople exist, and this is who consumers want to buy from!

The best news we can reiterate from our opening chapters is that this kind of sales approach cannot be faked – it's only open to the good guys.

Product knowledge is certainly important to consumers; in fact, knowledge-related answers comprised 14.02% of the responses. **However, 94.5% of all responses relate to the seller's soft skills and how they treat their customers!**

When we reorganized the responses based not on personal attributes – values, personality traits, or style – but behaviors or teachable skills, the data again supports a customer-centric approach in a major way.

The macro trends on important selling traits or behavior, in order, are;

- Focus on the customer and their needs: 92.1%
- Know your product or service and its value proposition: 14%
- Create a relaxed, comfortable, low-pressure environment: 13.4%

In our experience, most sales training programs are built around product knowledge, overcoming objections, and hitting numbers. According to our extensive survey, there seems to be quite the gap between how sales professionals are being trained, and how their eventual customers want to buy. This is why we needed to write this book!

In short, the survey and this brief but crucial chapter can be summarized into three main points:

1. The customer, not the product or service, is the focus of the conversation and the buying process.
2. The more the salesperson listens to and discovers about the customer, the better they can adapt and cater their approach to each customer's individual needs, which is exactly how our customers tell us they want to make their purchase decisions.
3. We sales professionals are there to be a resource; a veritable fountain of knowledge when it comes to our product or service and its value proposition. Even more importantly, we are there to be of service of our potential customers, always acting in their best interests.

It's okay to make a profit, even a very healthy markup, as we take care of our clients; but it's not okay to manipulate, push, or force a sale out of someone who doesn't legitimately want or need our services. Further research sheds light into the psychology of buyers, and why they chose their ultimate solution and provider.

- 70% of people make purchase decisions to solve problems. 30% make decisions to gain something[15]
- 95% of buyers chose a solution provider that "Provided them with ample content to help

navigate through each stage of the buying process"[5]

Take care of your customers, and sales managers and business owners take care of your sales teams, and they'll take care of the bottom line. While we believe it's essential to build your strategy and your approach based on customer input (such as our survey above), there's one success principle to sales we can never forget. We must *ask* for the sale!

The above notion may seem painfully obvious, but in our experience, 60% of sales professionals don't ask for the sale – they present their case and hope that clients offer to buy. While there are many ways to ask for a sale – and while it's critical that you do so in a way that allows you to be comfortable, confident, and authentic (see chapter three) – you must ask.

A few different ways of asking for the sale are below;

- Which of the options that we discussed do you feel best meets your needs and budget?
- How soon would you like to get started?
- Does this feel right? What does your gut (or heart) say about this purchase?
- It sounds like we're on the same page, can I wrap up the paperwork and take your payment information?
- I can send you an invoice this afternoon if you're ready.
- Have we earned the privilege of serving you?
- Are you ready to become part of the [ABC Company] family?

En route to a dinner party recently, one of our authors stopped in to a local wine merchant who had just opened (we love to support local business!). The owner said, "Nobody leaves my store empty-handed; that means I didn't do my job. What can I help you with?" Two bottles of wine and a case of beer later, his approach to selling is now immortalized in a book!

We've also experienced numerous ways to navigate those awkward moments when a client is clearly deciding, and we have no more evidence to add to our business case. Many sales trainers teach overcoming objections, but we've chosen a different approach.

In our experience, when any sales training program comes to overcoming objections, there's a noticeable shift of energy in the room. This is when the kind of authentic sales leaders we're trying to cultivate feel like they are hard selling or trying to get people to buy something they don't want or need.

Rather than closing techniques, we prefer clarifying questions, such as;

- Is there anything you're not 100% clear on, comfortable with, or sure about with respect to this purchase?
- What's getting in the way of you feeling great about making this purchase today?
- What more can I do to make this a very easy decision for you?

As noted above, the key is listening, and in many cases, this will involve you having to stay silent for a moment. We fully understand this is harder than it sounds, however, if you do not give your customer time to think you are back on the path of pushing versus guiding.

Questions like the above serve to empower the customer and simplify the purchase decision. Rather than a sale that's met with buyer's remorse, sales professionals who adopt these strategies will have customers raving about their experience and referring their networks. It really does become win-win selling.

Now that we've identified who your customers are, and how they want to buy from you, it's time to shift the focus to how to find more of your ideal customers.

CHAPTER FIVE
Pages Into Points

- ❖ Customers know how they want to buy. The people have spoken, and their number one piece of advice for us is to listen and understand their needs before suggesting anything
- ❖ When it comes time for us to make our offer, it should be as a process, in the form or advice, after a series of discovery questions and a natural back-and-forth conversation.
- ❖ As business owners and sales managers, we have historically been training product knowledge and closing techniques to a group of professionals whose most valuable skills are listening and asking powerful questions. Time to change our approach!

Chapter Six

Find your customer – and help them find you!

We've spent an entire chapter painting a detailed picture of your ideal customer avatar, and another on how they want to buy. Now it's time to examine how distinct stages of the buying cycle affect how we as sales professionals craft our client acquisition strategy.

Depending on the type of purchase, consumers make their decisions in different ways. If you're thirsty for a cola, for instance, you have four primary decisions:

1. What brand or type of cola do I want?
2. How much do I want (what size)?
3. Where can I purchase said cola?
4. How much am I willing to pay?

If our needs become more complex, we have more decisions to make and our buying cycle becomes longer (at least, it requires more decisions). Consider the largest purchase in most people's lives: a new home. The decisions that lead to a happy new homeowner might look something like;

1. Why do I want to move?
2. How does this affect what type of home I want to buy?
3. What amenities do I need access to? (grocery stores, schools, hospitals, parks,

recreational facilities, major roadways, churches, and more)

4. How far away is it from my place of work?
5. How safe is the neighborhood?
6. How does my lifestyle affect my purchase? (some homeowners opt for condos, so they don't have to mow the lawn, others may want a massive yard that is professionally landscaped)
7. How many bedrooms and bathrooms do I need?
8. Sun-chasers or those looking to avoid overexposure may decide their ideal home is based on sun exposure – a south facing backyard to soak up the sun (in the northern hemisphere) or eastern to enjoy a warm morning coffee but not burn all afternoon.
9. How many cars can fit in the garage?
10. Do I want a fully developed basement, or would I prefer the opportunity to develop one to my own specifications?
11. What kind of views are available, and how important is that to me?
12. Is a patio or balcony important?
13. What is the layout of the house?
14. Color scheme?
15. Does my home (or condo) have (within or communally) a fitness facility? Media room? Bar?
16. What appliances come with the home?
17. How do each of the above affect the ultimate purchase price?
18. How noisy is the neighborhood, and what kinds of noises? (for instance, construction, traffic, or kids playing – a young couple with

children may have different tolerance for some of these noises than retirees)

19. How busy is the traffic, and how safe is it for children to play outside? Parents with young families might want to live on a quiet cul-de-sac more than on a busy main street.

There could be many more variables when purchasing a home, vehicle, business, or other major purchase. In general, as consumers we buy through distinct phases that marketing professionals have dubbed the marketing funnel. In more recent years, sales and marketing professionals and academics have also measured customer behavior as a journey to be understood over the longer term in what is known as a "customer journey map."

We will examine both concepts as they relate to buying behavior, and how this should dictate our selling strategy. First, let's explore the more traditional marketing funnel.

Figure 6.1 Traditional Marketing Funnel

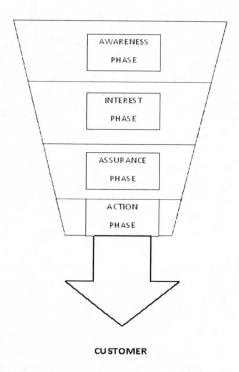

AWARENESS
PHASE

INTEREST
PHASE

ASSURANCE
PHASE

ACTION
PHASE

CUSTOMER

The above image represents potential customers as they first encounter a product or service. First, they discover your offering. They see an ad, meet someone at a party saying good (we hope) things about you, or they read about your work in a magazine related to your industry. In short, they become **aware** of you.

To maximize the effectiveness of this approach, it's imperative that the marketing and/or sales professional understands what activities drive the desired result. Then, understand what leads to conversion where the potential customer is moving deeper through the funnel en route to the action phase.

While some customers may enter at the bottom of the funnel ("My brother bought his home stereo here and I just had to have it"), a clear understanding of how potential customers move through each level of the funnel is critical to help sales professionals formulate effective strategies. This process is called lead nurturing. It's an important strategy because nurturing leads results in 20% more opportunities on average, and nurtured leads make 47% larger purchases than non-nurtured leads.[9] Furthermore, lead nurturing emails generate an 8% Click-Through Rate (CTR) compared to general email sends, which generate just a 3% CTR.[5]

If the above statistics weren't motivation enough, lead nurturing emails get between four and ten times the response rate when compared to standalone email blasts.[16] Companies that nurture leads make 50% more sales at a cost of 33% less than non-nurtured leads.[17]

Table 6.1 summarizes several strategic initiatives, metrics to measure effectiveness, and conversion tactics for each stage of the funnel.

Table 6.1: Marketing and sales initiatives through the funnel

Stage	Strategies	Metrics	Conversion Tips
Aware-ness	Guest blog writing Guest subject matter expert (SME) on podcast Social media marketing Mainstream media ads News/ magazine advertorial Billboard or poster ads Search Engine Optimization (SEO) tools	Reach, new followers Views, comments, shares Calls (A/B testing) Unique website views/ clicks	A/B test two different messages with different phone numbers to track effectiveness. Track web analytics when you advertise.
Affinity (Interest)	Free download Free webinar Web Summit Discounted or free initial service Email opt in on website SEO tools	Downloads Click-through rate Webinar or web summit attendees Redeemed coupons/ trial service vouchers Email opt-ins	Track survey or email open rates A/B split test on offers or different ads
Assurance	Content marketing Focus groups Live events	Open rate via email platform (e.g. Mailchimp or Benchmark) Event attendees Click-through rates Conversion rates	FAQ section on website - establish expertise Video and written testimonials
Action	Time limited sale Limited run offers (limit 10 people per webinar, etc.) Free gift to take next action (time limited)	Sales Conversion rates Attendees Click-through rates	Money back guarantee Value add gifts Limited time offers

It's very important to ensure that effective metrics are associated with each level of the funnel to understand what's working and what's not. We often hear, "I spent thousands on my website, and it's not making an impact on our sales!"

We must remember that a website (unless you're Amazon or eBay) is primarily a marketing asset. Most websites exist to drive awareness and then affinity of a brand, as opposed to direct sales. If we want to measure whether our website is doing its job, we should be measuring its effectiveness using key performance indicators (KPIs) from those phases, such as unique web visits, time spent on each page, number of pages visited, email opt-in rates, number of downloads, and metrics like these.

While the traditional marketing funnel gives a very thorough view of customer acquisition phases, it does so from a company-centric view. That is, the traditional marketing funnel tends to lead sales executives to ask questions like, "Where is the customer in our funnel and how can we move them along?" While useful, we feel that a better question tends to be, "How do my customers buy, and how should this impact our strategy?"

When we take this expanded, customer-centric view of purchasing behavior, we come up with a more in-depth (and we feel useful) tool called the customer journey map. The customer journey map is a map of the touch points a company may have with a potential customer: From research and buying to service delivery and upselling or even losing the customer. When a sales professional or company understands how each interaction with a customer relates to the likelihood of acquiring, retaining, and upselling to that customer, they can operationalize every aspect of what they do – and the results are astounding.

Figure 6.2 below outlines a hypothetical customer journey map for a financial planner. As was the case with the traditional marketing funnel, not every customer will go through each phase. Demonstrating a case study through all phases is helpful to understand each aspect of your customers' buying journey. This in turn affects your sales strategy, like knowing what to start, stop, or continue to see better results.

Figure 6.2: Sample Customer Journey Map

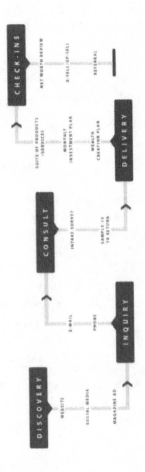

In this example, this financial advisor has three main ways that her customers can find her; her website, her social media channels, and an ad she took out in a magazine that was popular among her ideal customer avatar (see chapter four).

Through her own experience, and a series of interviews with professionals who had a financial advisor, she knew that people who strongly consider hiring a financial advisor reach out over the phone or email. She spent time working on her voicemail script and knew exactly what she'd say when answering the phone. For example: "Sarah the wealth generator, how may I help you today?"

In her market research, Sarah discovered that all advisors offer a free initial consultation, and they cover an overview of services provided that includes a future projection of what clients might accumulate in ten or 20 years with her help. Sarah's company has a proprietary software that demonstrates compound return rates on monthly pre-authorized contributions (PAC) to show her clients what they can achieve. Emailing the projection at the end of each meeting, with a few recommendations and history of the investments she'll recommend, leads to tremendous conversion rates from her potential clients.

In the delivery of her services, Sarah has found that providing quarterly portfolio updates and semi-annual check-ins with her clients has worked the best to provide her clients with peace of mind with their investments. Sarah has found that peace of mind and a growing portfolio have been the two most significant factors in retaining her clients.

During her semi-annual check-ins, Sarah goes through a review of her clients' net worth, at which time she asks how satisfied her clients are. She recommends larger monthly contributions (upsell), or new investment, insurance, or other financial products (cross-sell). These are the two key strategies to lift a customer's lifetime value (CLV), one of the most significant metrics any business can measure.

The above illustration is a straightforward example of a customer journey map. The more moving pieces your business has, and the more product or service features a customer can choose, the more complex the customer journey map becomes. The more complex your business, the more important the exercise becomes for you to anticipate and meet your clients' or customers' needs.

Try laying out the distinct steps, or phases, to the journey your customers take, and how this should inform your strategy. If you're not sure, chapter four discusses the value of focus groups and how your ideal or prospective customers can help you make better decisions with your business (or career).

CHAPTER SIX
Pages Into Points

- ❖ Customers typically go through a buying process when they make their purchase decisions.
- ❖ Businesses have typically understood the buyers' journey from inside out – 'how does someone come into our business?'
- ❖ Contemporary research and best practices are shifting to meet the customer where they are rather than trying to change their behavior.

Chapter Seven

The art of networking

"Everybody knows how important first impressions are. But not everybody knows that the 'first impression' is actually only a seven-second window upon first meeting someone."[18] - *Anna Pitts*

While the previous chapters have largely built a macro sales strategy, many sales professionals work for an organization rather than leading its strategy or owning the company altogether. Even if you are the Vice President of Sales for a Fortune 500 company, there will always be the need for face-to-face, eyeball-to-eyeball networking.

For those of you running your own business that is not entirely online, your entire sales strategy (and business success) might hinge upon your networking skills. If the last few chapters have taken a 50,000-foot view of sales in your business, this chapter is all about what to do when there's a potential lead that's two-feet in front of you. First, let's consider who you are networking with. In our experience there are three distinct groups to consider, and each will require a slightly different approach.

1. Direct Networking. Networking directly with your ideal customer base. Put another way, we could call this one-to-one networking.

2. Referral Networking. Networking with potential referral sources and distribution channels that deal with your customer base. When we form trusted relationships with a

great referral partner, it can be as effective as 100 networking events. A referral partner who really wants to see you succeed can be life-changing for a business!

3. Supplier Networking. Networking with suppliers or providers of products to your customer base. When we form close-knit or exclusive relationships with key suppliers, we can often create a competitive advantage within our business. A landscaping company who forms an exclusive regional agreement with Duradek, the popular maintenance-free vinyl deck solution, may find their sales skyrocket. Instead of having to win one customer over at a time through a bidding process, they might land several customers seeking a no hassle deck, who can only buy certain products through them. In this sense, supplier networking is akin to one to 1000 networking.

As you can see, your approach to each of these conversations will change based on the networking level. However, the following will give you a good baseline to help move you forward in the right direction.

Places to network

The world is a very large place and it can be scary to think where to start networking, so we've listed our top areas to start – depending on your business model.

- Chamber of Commerce

- Business Journal Clubs

- Networking Clubs

- Meetup Groups

- Personal Betterment or Educational Opportunities

- Private Clubs

- Civic Organizations

- Professional Associations

- Charity and/ or Non-Profit Organizations

- Sporting or Cultural Events

In some parts of the world, there's a large percentage of community-minded leaders who volunteer their time to support those around them. Find something you're passionate about. Offer your greatest skill set and connect with like-minded individuals, who, over time, you can add to your "Love Army™ (see Chapter Eight)."

Networking Events

They key to all networking events is mindset, and that starts from the moment you decide to register. At the time of registration set a solid and tangible intention for the event and start planning to achieve this. If your intention is to connect with ten new leads to initiate or grow your network, then this will help remind you that the time invested is valuable; thus, you're less likely to hang around chatting with those you already know.

For those who are more introverted, try reframing networking events from a necessary evil to an opportunity. How much would you pay to skip the RFP process and connect directly with the president of the company? That may be exactly what you are doing at your next networking event!

What to consider when networking

Why this event or activity?

Depending on your location you could attend a networking event almost every day of the week, so consider the value of each event before investing your valuable time and money. The following are questions to consider before attending a networking event:

i.   Are your ideal customers going to attend?
ii.   Are your referral sources going to attend?
iii. Are your supplier sources going to attend?

If none of the above are attending, then why are you if it is for networking purposes?

1. **Create a plan**

If you fail to plan, then you plan to fail.

If you haven't noticed, we're big believers in planning for success and not just waiting for it to happen – attending a networking event is no different. Create a simple worksheet, like the one below, prior to each event so you have a clear plan of what you want to achieve and how you are going to make it happen.

Networking Plan to Win worksheet

o Name of event:
o Date/ Time/ Location/ Cost of event:
o Attendees: Direct/ Referral / Suppliers
o Aim of event. What would you like to see
   happen at the event? That is;

- Connect with three new contacts on
  a deep level

- Find one feature about each person
  that makes them unique and
  memorable

- Find one thing you can do to serve
  and support

- Make every conversation all about
  the person you're meeting

o Reflection after the event:
o Was the aim of the event achieved? (If not,
   why not?)
o Return on time?
o Remember to factor in your prep time and
   follow up time after the event (Total time
   invested/ Outcome = Return on time)
o Return on investment?
o Remember to factor in your total cost of the
   event; that is, travel, parking, your time for
   prep/ event/ follow up, and expenses for the
   actual event (Total cost/ Outcome = Return
   on investment)
o What would you do different next time?
o Be very critical at this stage to ensure future
   success

2. Be prepared

Be organized and prepared mentally and physically
for networking success. Below are many of the topics
that come up regularly with networking, along with
practical suggestions.

Organized

- ❖ Time management
  - o Prepare for the event in advance
  - o Leave enough time to get to your event on time and remember to account for traffic and parking
- ❖ The pitch
  - o Your pitch is a quick summary of who you are and what you you've accomplished in your career, including your objectives. It's a crucial and effective tool to your networking success. You'll know your own pitch very well because you've practiced it many times and should be prepared to present it when you're asked what you do.
  - o Chapter 9 covers how to create an impactful pitch
- ❖ What to bring with you
  - o Pen and paper
    - ▪ Record contact information of those that did not bring a business card
    - ▪ Take notes with respect to the guest speaker
    - ▪ Even though you can record this information on your phone, we are trying to limit distractions
  - o Business cards
    - ▪ Business cards: Never leave home without them!
    - ▪ When we meet someone for the first time and they share their business card, we have already learned something about the person we are

meeting, before any words have been exchanged.

- This is your calling card and must impress every time. Distributing quality business cards is equally important as how you dress – first impressions are lasting.

- Develop a system when handing out your cards at events. Perhaps wear an outfit with pockets with cards you dispense in the right pocket, those you receive in the left. For women, you may assign a similar system using your handbag, or carry a palm-size card holder or wallet. Handing out someone else's card in error or having to cross the room to retrieve your card, wastes time and looks less than organized.

❖ Buddy up
  o Not everyone is comfortable carving out fresh new conversations with strangers. If this describes you, then invite an extroverted friend to come along to a networking event. You can join conversations that you're comfortable with and grow your confidence at your own pace.

Mental

☐ Stay positive by resisting the tendency to be negative when stress is high.

☐ When in the company of all others, maintain a positive vibe. The more positive

98

communications you have with those around you, the more your body's positive energy permeates your surroundings and mirrors back on you. It's true – this really works!

☐ Be well versed on global trends. With technology at your fingertips, you have every reason to be informed about what's happening in the world. Remember: You're not required to have an opinion, but to share a tidbit of knowledge that may spark interest in others. This is the best place to ask questions, and perhaps learn more about a new topic. You'll know when your opinion is of any interest when you are asked.

Physically

● Stay healthy ... in every way. Building out your business and sales targets can be one of the most stressful times of your life. Try to carve out at least 10 minutes every day to nurture your health and well-being: go for a walk, play with your kids or your pets, work out, enjoy your sport, practice yoga, meditate or ponder over a cup of tea in the sunshine, run a hot bath, weed your garden ... you get the idea. Whatever this activity is, it should bring you a sense of calm and self-reward. Without planning, these are the first activities to fall away and the most challenging ones to re-establish. Make this a commitment and part of your daily routine. Look at this time as an investment in resisting negative energy, and establishing a reserve of positive energy that will grant you greater work capacity over others.

- Nutrition is another very important element of staying healthy. Make careful choices in how you nourish your body. The quality of food you ingest will affect your level of energy.

Dress

This is one of the biggest stumbling blocks for people who attend networking events. WHAT DO I WEAR????? Is it business, casual, business casual, cocktail, black-tie? It is important to dress for the occasion, but at the same time it is ok to still have your own style within reason. Showing up in jeans to a black-tie event will not sit well with the organizer and vice versa.

Find out from the organizer what the dress code is for this event and then plan accordingly from there. Don't overthink it, and simply be you.

Dress to impress. This does not mean you must break the bank on the latest fashion trends. You must, however, coordinate your outfit with precision and thought.

Dress for success. All great fashion consultants will advise on investing in at least one key piece of clothing per season and mixing this piece with your existing wardrobe.

But what do I do if I don't have the funds to go out and buy that new suit/ dress etc.? Don't worry – many are in the same situation, but that's no excuse not to find a solution. We recommend the following in situations just like that, which have great success.

Consignment and thrift stores. Yes, that's right, your solution is right here at a fraction of the price. While many of these consignment stores vary in quality; every major center has them, so it's worth your time to investigate. If you know where the high-income earners live in a metropolitan area, chances are that consignment stores in those areas will carry some of this season's and last season's most popular pieces for a fraction of the retail (or original) cost.

3. Pre-event meetup

If you can see the guest list ahead of the event you should be connect with them prior. (They can become a warm lead as you have something in common; that is, the event). This can be as easy as connecting with them on Linked In and letting them know that you're looking forward to meeting them in person at such and such event. Alternatively, you can take it one step further and arrange to meet in person prior to the event to get to know the person better over coffee or lunch. Or, meet them five minutes prior to the event so you can walk in together, jump in a cab together, etc.

4. Show up

Over 20% of people that pay for networking events do not show up. What a waste! The truth is there are various reasons, but one of the main ones is fear. Fear, because they are not prepared, they do not have a plan and thus, they have no compelling reason to show up.

5. Be on time

Remember the reason for going to these events is to connect with possible customers or alliances that can connect you to your potential customers. It is vital that you maximize this opportunity; showing up late is not maximizing. If the event starts at 5:00 p.m. for networking, show up at 5:00 p.m. for networking, and not just before the start of the guest speaker section.

6. Networking etiquette

- Name Tags. If an event supplies name tags, make sure you wear one. We recommend placing it below your right shoulder so, when you meet a new face and shake hands, your tag is easy to read.
- Alcohol consumption and smoking are worth mentioning, too. Consider your ability to maintain a level of professional disposition, regardless of culture or protocols.
  - If you have a drink in your hand remember to hold it in your left hand so you can use your right hand to shake hands and it won't be wet from the glass.
- Food is often served at network events, but can also be a detriment. We recommend eating something before you go so you can focus on the event rather than your growling stomach. Remember, if you cannot shake hands, or your mouth is too full to have a conversation, your first impression may be less than impressive.
- Conversation
  - Positive attitudes rule! Regardless of your personal views on a topic, the best policy to impart a good impression is to reserve negativity for another time.

- o Stay away from controversial subjects.
- o Mirroring
    - o This is the behavior where one person consciously imitates the gesture, speech pattern, or attitude of another. This often occurs in social situations, which builds rapport. At the subconscious level, people feel less intimidated, more at ease and equal when conversing with someone who is similar to them. Successful mirroring starts from the very first moment we meet someone and shake their hand: where possible, a web-to-web handshake is most widely accepted. However, there will be situations that require a different approach, depending on culture or the possibility of meeting someone with a hand injury.
- o Eye Contact
    - o Give it freely and directly. However, keep in mind that where we are in the world will matter when it comes to eye contact. Different cultures may view eye contact as a form of aggression.
- o Listen up
    - o This empowering skill will provide you with a powerful advantage in many professional situations. Good listeners can reiterate and mirror what is important to others. Accepting what others say makes them feel important, validated and acknowledged.

6. Engage people you know

If you're new to networking, but have followed the steps above, then you'll know people there even if it's just through LinkedIn chats, etc. Worst case, if this happened to be a last-minute event, then the event staff should be your go-to people to connect with. It's their job to ensure a successful event and as such they will look after you if you ASK. Ask: "Hi, I'm looking to connect with X, Y, or Z type of person, who do you suggest I talk with first?" The event team is generally well connected and will point you in the right direction. Again, this only works if you ASK for help.

7. Turn off your cell phone

The biggest network killer by far is the cell phone. At all networking events you'll notice people using their cell phones thinking that it makes them look important. Realistically, it makes them look unapproachable. If you do need to make a sudden call or respond to an email, excuse yourself from the area and then come back when you are fully engaged again with the group. Your focus should be on the people around you so you can make meaningful connections. "But you don't understand, I'm on call and need to keep my cell phone on," or "I use my cell phone to track the contacts I chat with." We completely understand. We're simply suggesting that you need to understand that you're here to network, which should be your full focus. If you can't do that, then you're wasting your time.

8. Talk to people

Sounds crazy, right? We're serious. You're going to have to talk to people and be vulnerable. Just like your parents told you as a child, and you tell your children now, go introduce yourself, "Hi my name is Josh, what's yours?"

"But what do I say after I shake their hand and get their name???" Calm down, there are various ways, but here are some easy to remember tips to help guide you. Remember, this is not some random person at the bus stop, this is another person at a networking event trying to do the same thing as you – network.

A real conversation always contains an invitation. This is networking, not selling how wonderful you are. The aim here is to get to know other people and in return they will get to know you. We're fully aware this can be a scary thought, so try some of these icebreakers at your next event to get the conversation started:

- How do you know the host(ess)?

- What motivated you to attend this event?

- What are you looking to learn today from the speaker?

- Do you know other people that are attending today?

Here are some to avoid:

- Are you the decision maker for your organization?

- May I tell you more about what I sell?

- Do you know what time this event finishes because I really want to get out of here quickly?

Each one of our suggested questions is a threshold for expansion. Remember, the focus of the conversation should be on the person you're meeting and not on you and what you're selling.

Once the ice is broken your task now is to keep the conversation fluid and smooth to get to know your new connection better. To avoid stress, try this simple acronym that helps to keep conversations flowing "F.O.R.M." FORM is easy to remember and even easier to follow; thus, when you are nervous, this is an easy fall back.

FORM Conversation

F = Family

O = Occupation

R = Recreation

M = Motivation/ Message

Sample FORM questions

F = Family

- Do you live in the X area?

- If so, how long have you lived in this area?

- Why did you move here (or there)?

- Do you have children? How old are your children?

- How did you meet your partner? How long have you been together for?

O = Occupation

- Who are you representing here today?

- How long have you been with ABC Company?

- What do you do for ABC Company?

- What would you tell someone looking to start out in this profession?

- What is the best part of ABC Company / your role?

- If I was referring people over to you, who would be your ideal customer?

- What sort of challenges do you face?

R = Recreation

- When you're not working hard at A, B, C, what do you do in your spare time?

- How did you get into that?

- What do you have planned for the weekend?

- Are you watching the big game on the weekend?

- Do you have a favorite

  - show

  - movie

  - restaurant / food

  - sports team

- Do you belong to a volunteer organization?

- Does the organization where you volunteer need new members?

M = Motivation/ Message

- What brings you to this networking event?

- What other networking events do you normally attend?

- Are you a member or part of any charity or non-profit organization?

- What's important to you in today's ever-changing world?

When you're planning on ending your conversation and moving on, ensure you leave your guest with a message or statement that they will remember about you. Remember it will be a minimum 24 hours before they speak to you again, so you'll want that catch phrase or subject to stick with them. For example, consider something like the following:

- "It was great to meet you, Tammy! I have a note in my calendar to follow up on Monday to schedule a coffee, enjoy the rest of your evening!"
- "Greg, it was a pleasure speaking with you. I'll get you the name of that book I was talking about tomorrow when I can check my bookshelf. If you'd like to meet for coffee I can bring it for you to borrow."
- "Thanks again for the name of your accountant Stacey, I've been looking for a good one. I'll follow up after I reach out, and let's stay in touch."

Remember, conversations work both ways, and it's unwise to bombard people with questions and not give away anything about yourself. This doesn't mean that you boast about yourself, or for you to take center stage, it means that you're prepared to answer the same questions in a way that makes you likeable. Keep your answers short, positive and interesting; thus, if the person listening wants to know more they will ask. To help, write down some points next to each of the above questions so you have a well thought out answer when you are asked to keep the conversation flowing.

Relax and be yourself. Some events can be stressful. Learning how to approach these events feeling open and relaxed makes them enjoyable.

"If you focus on your curiosity and genuine interest in the other person, you won't have time to be nervous, self-conscious, awkward, self-critical, or anything

else. You will be too busy being interested in them."
[19] – Bob Burg

9. Collect contact info

The biggest mistake many networkers make is not collecting contact information from someone they meet; thus, they are not able to follow up after the event. Again, remember why you are there and ask for contact info. If they mention they do not have a business card, then it should not be a problem because you should have a pen and paper handy to record their details. Do not fall into the mistake of suggesting, "Here's my contact info and you send me yours." This means you'll have to wait to be contacted.

10. Follow up

"I don't want to be seen as a slimy sales guy and bug people." You should only feel like this if you're selling a product or service that you don't believe in. If you feel your product or service has value, then you're not bugging people by following up – you're helping them solve a problem. If you don't solve it, they'll find another product or service that will.

We will dive further into the follow up process later in the book, but it's vital that you understand this is just step one in the process of cultivating your contact towards becoming a customer, or referring customers to you. Here are a few pointers to get you started:

- ❖ Within 24 hours of the event:
  - o Send an invitation through social media to connect
- ❖ Within 48 hours of the event

110

- o Send a personal note that reminds your new friend of the conversation you had and invite them to meet in the next several weeks
- ❖ Ongoing
  - o Send them relevant information when you come across something you think they might be interested in
  - o If you made any promises at the event, ensure you follow through with them

Building rapport provides the opportunity to stay in touch six times, six different ways, over six months. This is an effective strategy to remain top-of-mind with your prospects, so that when it comes time to make a purchase or recommend a vendor, you're their first call!

Our next chapter is all about growing this sort of affinity with your network, and how to grow your network itself.

CHAPTER SEVEN
Pages Into Points

- ❖ Networking is key to success in sales in a world where buyers want to know, like, and trust their vendors.
- ❖ Choose to view networking as an opportunity rather than a necessary evil or a means to an end only.
- ❖ As with anything else, show up on purpose, following best practices to drive the outcomes you are seeking.
- ❖ Have fun – networking is just a social gathering with friends you haven't met yet!

Chapter Eight

Building your Love Army™

Catherine began using this technique when she worked at McGavin Foods early in her sales career. Her boss and mentor, Tim Fesik, taught her everything she needed to know about sales and high-touch client service. This method worked to grow her sales results and build her businesses over the years.

Reaching your target involves a simple formula. Start with the people who know and love you – we call them your Love Army. Ask them for information, referrals and advice in the area or industry you are interested in pursuing. It's important to realize that every person you meet along this route will be critical to your journey.

Step One

Start with the list of people who love you; that is, your Love Army. List them all – the people you can contact and ask for a one-hour meeting that will be all about you: Mom, uncle, sister, next door neighbor, yoga instructor … all of them. Let your Love Army know what you're trying to attract. You're seeking their information, referrals and advice. Say "yes" to all referrals that are given to you as opportunities to grow your network. Over time, expect up to five referrals from everyone in your Love Army.

You control the process! In most cases, your Love Army will want to make the introduction. Thank them for the referral and tell them you will make the initial contact. Remember to include their name. By taking this step out of their hands, you show initiative and avoid the possibility that they might get busy with their week and forget.

Use an Excel spreadsheet or CRM for a visual tracking system of your "Grow Who You Know™" process, procedure and success. **See Appendix B at the back of the book for the "Grow Who You Know**[TM]**" tool.**

<u>Step Two</u>

Do your research on the individual and their organization prior to contacting them. Research them using the Internet, LinkedIn, company website, annual report, and media releases.

Place the collected data in a file folder with the name of the person you're hoping to meet. When you do get that appointment, they'll be impressed to see that file in your hands.

<u>Step Three</u>

Plan your telephone communication for a time that will most likely be received positively:

- Avoid their first day of work after the weekend or holiday. They'll be catching up and may not want to be distracted.
- The best day is their second workday in the afternoon.
- Mornings between 7:30am and 8:30am before they get their day started.
- The last day of their workweek between 1:30 p.m. and the end of that day is also a good

time for many. When we're attempting to connect with decision makers, they typically remain in their offices to continue motivating their team. They, too, are thinking about the weekend and are more open to having an initial, non-pressured conversation.

- Have your calendar open and ready to go before you dial their number! If you're initiating the process, you must be prepared. You'll lose your own momentum when a prospect that you reach out to agrees to a meeting, only to have to wait for you to fire up your laptop and open your email calendar.
- If you do not reach your intended target – let's call her Sarah – but instead reach her assistant, James, be sure to add James, and his role, to your Grow Who You Know tool.

Email and LinkedIn messaging are suitable at any time and allow the recipient to respond on their own time.

Step Four

Record your call on your Grow Who You Know tool such as an Excel spreadsheet, CRM database, etc.

Keep a running check of your promises to return calls, attend invitations to meet, coffee dates, and so on. Be precise, attentive, and diligent with your commitments.

Back to the Grow Who You Know tool: Mark down this day's mode of communication with Sarah, and that you connected with James again.

The next step is extremely important!

Again, follow through with your promises. Do whatever you stated you would do and make good on all intentions.

In Catherine's case, she met with James in person and brought along her award-winning butter tarts. James asked her if she wanted to see Sarah, who was in her office. Catherine said, "I appreciate the offer, but I came to say hello to you. I'll reach Sarah another time." Catherine gained a trusted and valued connection that day with Sarah's gatekeeper, James. She also honored Sarah by not unexpectedly interrupting her day.

Record your efforts in the Grow Who You Know tool: At this stage in the process, Catherine has made a new friend in James. He'll likely extend every effort to ensure that, if Sarah is in the office, she'll take the call. If she is not available, then one last message will be left on her voicemail.

Step Five

When you finally make the connection, be dressed for success with research notes ready and your online calendar open. We recommend standing up for a call such as this; with all other background noises minimized and phone notifications turned off.

When is enough, enough? We recommend you try reaching an individual three times as shown in the examples above.

If you haven't been able to connect in person, leave a phone or email message saying you understand they are very busy and you will not contact them again, although you would enjoy meeting with them in the future. It's important to provide this closure so your communication is not left dangling.

<u>Step Six</u>

When you are successful in arranging a meeting with the referral, be organized.

- Have all your research information contained neatly inside a file folder, labelled with their name, and ready for reference.
- Bring the beverage or treat you promised.
- Have a list of questions handy. Remember, you may only have 10 minutes.
- Set your timer or keep an eye on your watch to keep track. At the nine-minute mark, thank them for the meeting and say that you see your time is up. In most cases, there is more time in their calendar to continue the meeting and let them decide if they wish to do so.

Here are some examples of what you might ask:

- What are the biggest opportunities for your company (or for you in your role) right now?
- What are the biggest hurdles or challenges in your business (or role) at present?
- What solutions have your tried in the past with respect to your challenges?

Of course, these are generic questions. Any of them can be made more specific, and infinitely more valuable, by catering your questions to your prospect based on your research. Remember chapter five, the goal is to understand their needs and goals so that you can recommend a perfect solution. Choose your questions ahead of time.

If your meeting is not with the decision maker, but rather someone your Love Army recommends because they work for the ideal company you're trying to do business with, then your goals are to build rapport and to learn. Learn by asking questions which helps to build rapport. Build rapport to the point where you can add Jim in accounting to your Love Army, who may very well direct you to Taylor in procurement who is the ultimate decision maker.

When rapport building is the primary objective, the focus must be kept on the person you're meeting, not on you or your offering. You'll know when it's time to talk when you're asked. When that happens, ensure your answer is two minutes or less. Then be ready with your next question to turn the conversation back to focus on them.

Take notes during the meeting for future reference.

Step Seven

After the meeting: Add your notes in your Grow Who You Know tool. Send a note to thank them for their time, capturing some of the highlights of your discussion, and reiterating that you're available to serve and support them in the ways you may have discussed. Keep them top of mind by sending them articles or videos that they may find of interest. Six times, six different ways, over six months.

You're now building a foundation of trust, respect and integrity with the goal of moving your new contact to your Love Army list.

Final Step

Always go back to water the well. Remember to thank the person who gave you the initial referral. They will almost always start thinking of others they can refer you to. Your Love Army wants to be there for you and you need to make it easy for them.

CHAPTER EIGHT
Pages Into Points

❖ Everyone you meet through networking and prospecting is important. Never underestimate the power of the 'gatekeepers' in any business.
❖ Just as you would with your product or service, find a way to differentiate yourself through your approach to business.

PART THREE

KNOW YOUR STUFF

Chapter Nine

Your Positioning Statement (a.k.a. Your Elevator Pitch)

"We're in the paper business" is a lot less convincing and appealing than "We help your ideas come to life."

"I'm an accountant" sounds nowhere near as valuable as "I empower business owners to make great financial decisions and to harness the potential of their business."

Knowing what you do differently and better than the competition, and how you differentiate yourself in a competitive marketplace (or even as an employer) is key to establishing, enhancing and delivering on your competitive advantage.

Put another way, your positioning statement is your answer to the question, "why should I listen to you?" before it is asked.

Answering a few small questions, ideally with team and customer input, can help galvanize what may otherwise be an intangible, unintelligible ramble about what you think you do. Below are a few key questions and statements about your product or service to help make the intangible more concrete and more memorable with your target audience.

Organizational Pitch (My company does...)

- Core Purpose: "Why our company exists, other than making money"

- Mission Statement: only include it if it's not 'fluff'; saying "We're a collaborative and innovative leader in sustainable best practices who help make our community better" is a run-on sentence that doesn't say anything and can't be operationalized
- Core Values: "Who we are; what we stand for"
- Core Product, or Core Competencies: "What we do/ what we do differently or better than anyone else"
- Your credibility: this could be 25 years in business, or it could be your credibility as a professional within your own industry
- Your motivation: corporately, this may be your purpose or mission. Personally, this may be the reason you started your business, or the type of work you'd like to do or type of company you'd like to work for
- Target Market: "Who we serve/ sell to"
- Placement: "How we get our product/ service into our customers hands"

Your 'hook'. The unique, catchy, or memorable aspects of your product or service, or your unique skills or attributes as a professional. In our coaching business, it's the peace of mind we promise as well as the notion of reinvigorating a leader's or owner's passion (see Stan's pitch below).

If there are any other key defining or differentiating elements, such as physical experience of your space, if your price structure puts you ahead of market, being the only provider in your region, etc., then add those elements here. Otherwise, the above elements serve to start a conversation of who you are and what you do. It's in the above details, and the strategy, that most businesses find their unique position in the marketplace. This is what a potential customer or a potential investor is asking when they say, "So, what do you do?"

Personal Pitch (I do…)

Purpose: Your personal pitch is an impromptu opportunity for you to express a quick summary of who you are, what sets you apart from your competition, and to entice your listener to ask questions and learn more about you.

Three Main Components:

1.   Who you are: Why should they listen to you?

2.   What you do: What are you an expert at, or passionate about?

3.   Who you serve: How do you apply your unique skill set?

Here are some examples of pitch foundations developed by some of our friends:

Catherine: "I'm a 30-year entrepreneur, passionate about connecting people and organizations across the globe that I believe in. I look forward to applying my expertise and experience to international community development."

Stan: "I'm a business and performance coach driven to help 'triple bottom line' focused leaders maximize their potential and their returns."

Liane: "Over the past decade, I've developed my skills in the areas of writing, editing, publishing and language. I empower others to maximize their messages with minimal words, the results of which bring clarity and advancement."

Here are even tighter versions of perfected pitches that will leave the listener wanting more:

Catherine: "I connect people across the globe that I believe in – and sometimes I make money at it. I look forward to serving and supporting."

Stan: "I help values-based leaders gain the peace of mind to sleep better at night and the inspiration to wake up the next day ready to make their dreams a reality."

Liane: "My passion for perfecting the spoken and written message has helped both me and those with whom I collaborate to achieve clarity and voice."

MAKE IT YOURS

In our networking events we routinely help professionals craft and hone their pitches. Sometimes it's a tweak here, an edit there, or a few word suggestions. Sometimes, it's a complete overhaul or cutting 90% of the 'fluff' to focus on the 'meat'. In any case, however polished, professional, or intriguing a pitch may sound, it should be something you can make authentically yours.

One of our attendees first attempts at her pitch was something like the following;

"My name is Beth (not her real name), and I have a 15-year history in engineering. I have received a lot of recognition for my ability to improve processes and systems, and I have a very analytical approach to project management and implementation. My superiors are always fond of my work and they have mentioned that I help make their jobs easier. I am also very attentive to budgets, timelines, and resources as I implement better systems and processes."

Beth's pitch was a lot longer than that, but you get the point. One suggestion to simplify her pitch was, "CEO's love me because I think processes are sexy." The whole room cheered and thought our suggestion nailed it – except for Beth! Extremely introverted, proper, and professional – this was something she could never own with confidence. A better suggestion, once we learned this, was, "I help make executives lives easier by supporting them with seamless processes."

In summary, no matter how good your pitch looks on paper, it must be YOUR pitch – you must be able to say it confidently, authentically, and with authority.

PRACTICE, PRACTICE, PRACTICE!

Once you've secured the three elements, you'll become adept at altering your content as required. Your pitch will become more comfortable the more you practice it. It'll be important to create several different pitches, depending on where you are and with whom you are connecting. Be ready to change it on the fly.

Your pitch should be practiced enough to be top of mind and conversationally roll off your tongue, but not so rehearsed that you come across as robotic or "salesy" (even if you are selling).

NO HISTORY PLEASE

When people are asked what they do, they typically tell the history of how they arrived where they are today. Do not do this! Keep your conversation forward moving and positive.

Imagine you ask someone why he's at the biker club gathering and he rambles on about how he used to ride a Honda, but it became boring and now he'd really like to find a Harley. No!

It's better to start with the future in a specific way … "I'm looking for a 1961 Harley-Davison," or "I'm looking for a job in human resources in energy," or "I'm looking for information about sales and marketing in energy supply companies."

STAY POSITIVE

We encourage you to keep your entire conversation with contacts and potential prospects positive – especially when you talk about your company's track

126

record and current or previous customers. Otherwise, you'll represent yourself as a negative person.

BE CREATIVE

Most people we encounter miss their opportunity to open new conversations by bypassing their pitch. Instead of "I help values-based leaders gain the peace of mind to sleep better at night and the inspiration to wake up the next day ready to make their dreams a reality," they simply open with, "My name is Stan, and I am a business coach." To help you move away from name and position introductions, here are a few more clever pitches to consider.

Title	Creative Pitch
• Carpenter	"I build dream homes"
• Dentist	"I'm in the smile business"
• Jeweler	"I've been getting girls next-door gala ready since 1997"
• Accountant	"I teach people to save $5,000 in taxes in 45 minutes"
• Server	"I'm a professional conversationalist who sometimes goes over the dinner special"

ALL ABOUT YOUR AUDIENCE

Your pitch is very brief for a good reason: the rest of the conversation should be focused on finding out about the other person. Where does he work? What does she like about her role? What are the challenges? What is he proud of? How did she get her first job in the energy sector?

All people naturally love to talk about themselves. While asking them questions and listening carefully to their answers, you're learning more and more about their unique challenges, which helps you position your offering as their ideal solution. Understand their needs, then position your solution, just as our survey reveals in chapter five.

Tip: Try to engage whomever you're talking to with questions first. Most people are more willing to listen to you after you've listened to them. By showing genuine interest in who they are, they'll become more interested to learn more about you.

THE GOAL

Even if you're looking to land a new client, your pitch is not a sales proposition or call to action. The goal of your pitch is to ignite a conversation. The likelihood of being hired or contracted based on your opening statement is virtually zero. A clever, well-crafted pitch can open a conversation by grabbing the client's or customer's genuine interest. If they're genuinely interested in you at the onset of a conversation, you have the opportunity to tell your story so they can see you for the true professional you are.

The more interested they are on the way into a conversation, the more likely they'll remember you afterwards and that multiplies your chances of moving through the purchase vetting process towards an eventual sale!

DID YOU NAIL IT?

As mentioned, the goal of your pitch is to ignite a conversation. We use the word "ignite" deliberately to convey emotion, enthusiasm, as one would say to another who appears to be on a roll, "You're on fire!"

This means there's some excitement to the conversation! One way you can tell whether your pitch worked is by the type of questions you get in response. No question often means no interest. "I'm sorry, what do you do again?" means that your pitch wasn't clear. Questions like, "How do you do that?" or "How long have you done that for?" or "Where did you learn to do that?" are all indicative of interest, even being impressed.

CHAPTER NINE
Pages Into Points

- ❖ Your positioning statement is your answer to the question, "why should I listen to you?" before it is asked.
- ❖ Your pitch should revolve around who you serve, and how you uniquely solve their problems, rather than your background and credentials

---

Chapter Ten

Success is a system

One major area where many sales professionals struggle is in the implementation and consistent execution of effective systems. Systems tend to increase income and predict future success. There are many reasons sales professionals may struggle with systems, but the main ones in our experience are:

- Lack of organization or time management
- Fighting the system because most true hunters, and even many farmers, prefer a lot of autonomy and to do their own thing
- Lack of consistency or routine
- Lack of understanding of the benefits or ROI yielded through the consistent application of effective systems.

With effective systems, from the CRM management software we use to time management and follow up systems, we can increase the likelihood, frequency, and predictability of intended results. In short, we can systemize the success we seek. To do so, we suggest sales professionals organize their efforts in the following eight ways.

1. Organize your day from the start.

We're big advocates for the power of the morning routine. As Will Durant said, in a quote most often attributed to Aristotle[20], "We are what we repeatedly do. Excellence is not an act, but a habit."[21]

Our method for starting the day with purpose, and creating a GREAT day, is as follows;

Wake up early (before 6:00 a.m.) and follow our GRATE method.[22]

Gratitude: Begin the day by focusing on what you are most grateful for. This could be your job or business, your family, the country you live in, the freedom you enjoy, anything that moves you to a state of deep appreciation. When we start our days this way, we bring more positivity into our lives, and we're in a better position to see opportunities rather than the challenges and obstacles in our way.

Relationships: To ensure we create and maintain life balance as we pursue our professional goals, we recommend taking a mental inventory of the state of the most important relationships in your life every day. We can't stay mad at our spouse if we reflect on the state of our marriage or relationship every day. Even if we're missing our numbers one month, thinking about your spouse, your kids, or your best friends may be a great source of positivity to help begin your day on the right foot.

Achieved: When we've begun the morning with deep gratitude, and considered the relationships we're fostering, we find it a great practice to move the focus much more granular. The third step in our morning routine is to picture every important task, and every meeting, and create a vision of success for every single one. Set your ideal outcome, and then visualize that outcome is achieved. Visualize your sales meeting as a done deal, imagine your success with every phone call to prospects, and any other task that has been achieved, and at an amazing level at that.

Tweak: After scanning your day's to-do list, we find it's important to tweak your day. Have you overextended yourself and it's unlikely you'll execute fifteen things at an optimal level? Are there only three things on your list that you can easily achieve by noon? Add, subtract, or tweak your day accordingly to set yourself up for success.

Exercise: Finally, before you hit the ground running, hit the ground and run! Or lift weights, take a yoga or spin class, anything that gets your heart pumping, body moving, and that makes you healthier. Even stretching does wonders for the body on a day that you might be tired, sick, or sore from yesterday's workout.

As with any other routine, the above might not make you an instant success. However, when you add up the discipline of this powerful morning routine day after day, you will have the energy, commitment, perspective, and life balance necessary to conquer your industry and achieve just about any goals you set for yourself.

2. Organize your weeks in advance

Time is the one asset we can't get back, can't buy, and can't create more of. The most successful people on the planet seem to bend time and do more with their 24 hours than others. Elon Musk, for instance, has his day down to an almost exact science, scheduling his day in five-minute increments[23]. We recommend scheduling each week in advance such as a Thursday afternoon because you'll most likely

have a good idea of what you need to do by then.
Finally, we recommend reviewing your day each
evening to assess what you achieved, what you
didn't, and what you need to adjust for the next day.
Effectively, how you end your day is just as important
as how you started it.

3. Set aside time each week, if not each day,
   for new business development

Through our coaching practice, we get to see how
businesses, in various industries, go about selling. It
never ceases to amaze us how often sales
professionals fall into the trap of busy work and forget
to sell!

Of course, there's always paperwork to do, CRMs to
update, meetings to attend, and new products or
services to familiarize ourselves with – but selling
should always be at the core of what a salesperson
does.

We recommend operationalizing your business
development efforts. This might be done based on a
specific day – Tuesdays for follow up, Thursdays for
prospecting new leads, for instance – or it might be
every day.

Statistically, the suggested best times to **email are**:

- email prospects between 8:00 a.m. to 10:00
  a.m. and 3:00 p.m. to 4:00 p.m.[24]
- Tuesday emails have the highest open rate
  compared to other weekdays[25]
- Tuesdays also have the highest conversion
  rate, with 14.72% more sales being
  converted on a Tuesday than a Friday[26]

The best times to call are:

- Wednesdays and Thursdays, from 6:45 a.m. to 9:00 a.m.[24]
- Wednesdays and Thursdays from 4:00 p.m. to 6:00 p.m.[24]

The worst times to call are Mondays at 6:00 a.m. and Friday afternoons.[24]

Your specific ideal avatar may have different schedule patterns than the average employee or business owner. For instance, food and beverage staff often work Wednesday to Sunday instead of Monday to Friday; whereas first responders often work four days on; four days off schedules, including shift work.

For certain industries there are buying windows, and those windows need to be maximized.

- In the fitness Industry, there are three major spikes for sales: January (the New Year's rush), May (fit before summer) and September (the kids are back to school, parents can get back to their routines)
- For landscaping companies in the northern United States and Canada, the key selling seasons are spring (have your outdoor living space ready for summer party season) and fall (get it done before winter)
- For companies selling to government organizations, the fourth quarter of the year becomes a critical sales window when governments need to spend any remaining

budget lest their budgets be reduced the following fiscal year; and

- For companies selling to construction builders and contractors in northern climates, spring becomes the quintessential selling window, as summer is the prime construction season

In addition to maximizing selling windows throughout the week and at different times of the year, it's also essential to optimize our days. Jeb Blount refers to the standard business day as the "Golden Hours," and suggests that the greatest challenge for salespeople is to prevent non-revenue generating tasks from interrupting selling behaviors during these times[27]. Blount goes further to discuss the benefits of hyper-focused time. In one case example, he helped a tele-prospecting team go from less than 25 calls a day to averaging 29 calls in 30 minutes![27]

Distraction is the great killer of productivity. The simple antidote is to plan your most productive time (generally mornings) for your most productive tasks. Instead of scheduling your day haphazardly, block time throughout the day and week to focus on those tasks you know (or suspect) are going to be most critical to your business success. For example, Tuesdays and Thursdays from 8:00 a.m. to 10:00 a.m. for new prospecting.

Lastly, ensure that prospecting and business development efforts make their way into every day. Sales reps who try to cram before the end of a quarter, month, or year see terrible results. Success (or win rate) drops by 51.11% at the end of a month, with a corresponding decrease of 34.5% in deal size.[26]

4. Organize your efforts based on ROI

As Richard Koch points out in his book *The 80/20 Principle*[28], 80% of our efforts will yield less than 20% of our results. As such, it becomes critical to success to optimize our time by focusing on our highest priority or most urgent tasks.[28] This drives the previous point home: busy isn't the goal anymore. Busy might be counterproductive, and productivity is the real goal.

Two questions will help anchor your focus and productivity as it relates to the 80/20 rule Koch discusses[28].

First, why am I doing this? This may seem a simple question, but if the goal is to sell, and the task you're about to undertake doesn't aid in your sales efforts, why are you doing it? Of course, we are not condoning insubordination; rather, a concerted look at your efforts to maximize the percentage of time spent on productive sales activities.

Second, how am I doing? If the activities we undertake do correlate to sales, what is that correlation, and how are we performing? This could be calls per hour, prospects uploaded into your CRM, even door to door flyers handed out – put a number on your efforts and challenge yourself to raise the bar every day, week, month, and year.

Those who follow these two disciplines at a high level blow away their counterparts. According to research by Propeller[9], 8% of all salespeople account for 80% of all sales.

5. Organize your prospecting

Today, there are many tools that can be used to help you stay organized and follow up with possible customers. We could write a book just on the topic of CRM software and how to stay organized. For our purposes, here's a snapshot of how to use CRM software to maximize your prospecting productivity.

From free versions all the way to hundreds or thousands of dollars a month, CRM software does the same thing, but to various degrees of complexity. CRM systems consolidate customer information into a database so that the user can easily access and manage the data effectively. A great benefit of using a CRM is the ability to record all interactions with your customers, including email, phone, social media and various other systems, so no more sticky notes or multiple excel tracking sheets!

There are various levels of complexity. For instance, some CRMs include the ability to automate workflow processes. This automation includes systems like task management, calendars, date, time alerts, email tracking and reporting metrics. These reporting metrics can include everything from the number of calls made to predicting your revenue at the end of the month, quarter or year. Don't worry if you're not a savvy veteran when it comes to using CRMs; research by HubSpot[26] found that 22% of salespeople don't even know what a CRM is!

One of the most important features of a CRM is the ability to create deal stages (basically the marketing funnel or customer journey map discussed in chapter six). When a company knows their prospects' buying stages intimately, they can place all pending deals across the various stages, and this can guide their follow up initiatives.

A paper supplier might understand their customers' deal stages as follows;

I.   Prospect identified
II.   Prospect approached
III.   Meeting scheduled
IV.   Follow up sent
V.   RFP (request for proposal or request for pricing as the case dictates) obtained
VI.   Vendor shortlist
VII.   Quote sent
VIII. Contract signed (closed won in CRM terminology)

A prospect might find that three of the prospects approached in stage two never replied. This lets them know exactly what action to take, because the salesperson knows that the goal in stage two is to land a meeting to discuss their prospects' paper needs.

Three popular small to mid-sized systems are Hubspot, Zoho, and SAP, but there are numerous new contenders appearing daily. For the larger organization, four leading options are Salesforce, HubSpot, SAP and Oracle.

As with any software, it's only as good as the user executing the controls. With that it is worth bearing in mind these top tips for using any CRM.

A. **Learn how to use it**. This may seem obvious; however, a great majority of sales professionals skip this step, opting instead to go straight to inputting data and trying to figure it out as they go. They often end up wasting a huge amount of time and suffer needlessly by using this approach. According to HubSpot, 60% of their users have never used a CRM before.[29] With this being the case, it becomes critical for new users to take the time to learn the system. Considering that many CRMs have video guides and online tutorials, learning has never been easier. Learn how to make your CRM work for you!

B. **Make it your go-to software**. If you are using several programs for several distinct functions, you are likely wasting time and money. If you are going to use a CRM effectively you need to jump in with both feet. The saying "garbage in, garbage out" relates well here, meaning if the system does not have all the data, we cannot expect it to give accurate reports or assist us in closing more business. Most of the platforms now have plug-ins with all the other major software you use (that is, your email, your calendar, your social networks, your accounting system, etc.). In short, within your CRM, you have access to everything without needing to open another application.

C. **Your CRM needs to be part of marketing.** Many CRMs have their own data collections points, forms, etc., that you can embed into your website; they may even have their own landing page templates, which makes it a breeze to collect the data. Receive leads that are input directly into the system, which saves you time.

D. **Frequency of use.** Since this is your go-to software, your CRM should be opened every morning at the same time you open your email (some CRMs can also be your complete email system). The more you keep your data up-to-date the more your reports and projections will be accurate; therefore, aiding in the management of your sales process.

E. **Trust the system.** If you have a system, then trust it, stick to it, and then keep modifying it as you go along to refine it. This can be completed by using the CRM reports and see where your flaws are. If you do not have a system, you could be losing sales, customers, and your reputation. Companies that automate lead management see a 10% or greater increase in revenue between six to nine months.[30]

6. Organize your information

Chapter four dove into your ideal customer avatar. Chapter five added empirical research to the buying process. Chapter six unveiled the traditional marketing funnel and the customer journey map. If your business has these concepts flushed out well enough, your organization can begin to add rigor in the form of metrics. This becomes the backbone of business intelligence (BI) or customer intelligence.

With relevant metrics, we can accurately identify, describe, and locate (thus acquire) our ideal customer. We can track our cost of customer acquisition and create our budget from there. If we know our customer lifetime value (CLV) and cost of acquisition, we can create a budget to entertain and acquire customers. Not all customers are created equal, and, with the right metrics, savvy sales professionals can spend more time pursuing more valuable customers.

With great metrics, a business becomes empowered to hire better and understand the attributes proven to drive success. Companies can then enhance their onboarding and training programs, ensure the development of effective techniques and tasks, which becomes part of the daily routines for their teams.

7.   Organize your strategy

Every business is different. Even two direct competitors with near-identical products or services vying for the same customer base will likely choose different strategies to acquire them. Copying what other successful companies do will lead you, at best, to be almost as successful as they are. To lead an industry, individuals and companies must chart their own paths with unique, if not revolutionary, strategies.

Essential to setting your sales or business strategy is the business intelligence noted above; as measured against trying new things and then documenting the success of each strategy. To reiterate, time is the most limited resource. As such, effective sales organizations must establish routine check-ins of their strategies and associated results. Close rates, cost of client acquisition, customer lifetime value, and sales cycle length must be measured for every strategy you deploy. Additionally, the individual performance of each sales team member should be measured against established benchmarks and goals.

Whether each week, month, or quarter, your strategies must be measured against these benchmarks. Sales executives and business leaders must decide what to stop doing, keep doing, and what to start doing. Over time, this becomes a fluid process with only the strategies that produce results being kept.

One caveat to the "stop, keep, start" method is to ensure you've given a strategy enough time and input to measure the results before abandoning the strategy.

8.   Organize your future

One of the most unique problems we encounter in our coaching practice and our recruitment business is the *victim of our own success* gap. A sales rock star is promoted to sales leader, only to have their sales performance not replaced by the incumbent account representative. In other cases, a business is booming, but the owner wants to retire, and the business is not yet a turnkey solution for a prospective incoming buyer.

The *victim of our own success* gap is the same challenge of all great leaders: to replace oneself with someone even better. Therefore, systems are critical. You can't scale a business on personality or talent. A single high performer can negatively impact the valuation of a business; sophisticated investors know that if the rock star leaves, sales and revenue will drop. Even for a solo entrepreneur, sales success is far less likely predicted by talent or charisma than it is by work ethic and effective systems honed over time.

In short, the better your systems, the better your business, and the easier it will be for you to achieve that promotion, grow beyond your current role, or even sell your business for what you deserve. Build your business, or organize your career, from day one as though you may one day want to sell or get promoted.

Before you move on from this chapter, we suggest you stop and take an inventory of your systems. To help, we've placed a brief questionnaire at the end of this chapter. Because this is one of the more process- and detail- heavy chapters of the book, it's critical not to skip over these systems with a 'I'll get back to it later' mindset (because most people won't). Bookmark your page, and ensure your systems are set up and working for you before you go onto chapter eleven.

System	Currently using	Self score/ 10	Plan to improve
Morning routine			
Time management			
Performance measurement (KPI dashboard)			
Reviewing sales strategy success			
CRM			
Business Intelligence (data)			
Scaling/ succession plan			

Success is a system. How good is yours?

CHAPTER TEN
Pages Into Points

- ❖ Success leaves clues. If there is a company or person whose success you want to emulate, learn their behaviors and implement what they do. They are successful for a reason!
- ❖ Execution trumps perfection when it comes to success principles. It's better to execute a good plan with unwavering discipline than it is to try and perfect the plan before you get started.
- ❖ Systems should evolve over time. Execute with rigorous consistency – but always be open to learning a better way of doing things.

Chapter Eleven

The Anatomy of a Sale

By now you've gone on the journey to learn about who you are as a professional, who your customers are, how they want to buy, and also a set of effective systems to serve those customers at a higher level. Before we move to our final chapter, we want to apply all that you've learned against a road map of how an actual sale transpires so that all of the research, theories, and our experience can serve you in the most practical manner possible.

We would like to suggest that there are three parts, or phases, to the sale, though the timing, length, and details of each phase may vary widely based on your company, industry, or customer segment. Nonetheless, we would like to suggest that sales have the following three phases;

- Pre-sale phase

- Action phase

- Post – sale phase

Each phase has several components, which make up the sales road map we are suggesting. As we lay out each aspect of each sales phase, we want you to consider how comfortable you feel with each activity, and with driving the desired outcomes. The value in this chapter then, will be a handy reference guide to understand where you may excel, and where you might need improvement. From there, you can truly personalize your sales approach to your customer, and play to your strengths as well as tighten up any areas that might be leading you to lose sales.

Pre-sale Phase

The first part of chapter three covers a great set of questions going into a first sales meeting, for either B2B or business to consumer sales. In addition to researching your prospect and/ or their company as detailed in the third chapter, we also recommend the following steps in the pre-sale phase;

1. Review the deal in your CRM software or in your internal notes. What are the important deal specifics or milestones that have already occurred? What notes have you made to yourself regarding the names of your prospects' children, or their favorite baseball team or where they went to college?

2. Set your state. The second half of chapter three (page 47) teaches how we can optimize our physical and emotional state to show up as the best version of ourselves. Forgetting to do this is just as harmful as showing up to a big sales meeting in pajamas.

3. Arrive early. If you're on time to a sales meeting – you're late. Be there early so that you can get in state, stay in state, be the one to pay for coffee or at least grab a table. This is especially true if you work in an office, retail, or warehouse setting. Can you imagine your prospect beating you to your own place of work? Not professional. For larger organizations, or professionals who travel to meet their prospective customers, it's also critical to arrive early if you find

yourself in a new city and you're not familiar with Montreal's traffic patterns or parking availability (for instance).

4. Go over and above. Catherine is the queen of homemade butter tarts. She has brought them on many occasions (when she feels it's appropriate) to her prospect, or their receptionist, as mentioned in chapter eight). Stan was meeting with a business owner regarding growing her business. While the owners' bio on her own website gleaned some wisdom, in researching another prospect, he discovered that this owner did some part time work as a spin class instructor for his other potential client. The first owners' bio on the other owners' website was much more helpful – Stan learned that she was a pushover for Swedish Berry candies. In their first meeting, he was able to buy coffee, and then nonchalantly offer, "Oh, I also brought you these". His prospect was shocked (and thrilled)!

Action Phase

We define the action phase as all of the interactions, dialogue, and processes that occur while you are customer facing. For many professionals, this can be a single meeting or even an unplanned interaction as may be the case in retail. For other salespeople, this could be several meetings, and these meetings may occur in person, online, over the phone, or a combination of all of the above.

Our suggestion is to read the following section, and all of its components, and apply it to the specifics of your company, customer, and industry. For those professionals who find a disconnect between serving the customer and excelling at sales, this is the phase where you're most likely to find an opportunity to tweak your process for better results.

While no two sales meetings may look alike, an action phase road map often follows the following 11 steps;

1. Greeting. We all know how important first impressions are, but your greeting goes beyond that. When your prospect first arrives, whether it's your first meeting or fifteenth, they should always feel welcomed, and that they are your only priority for the entirety of your time together. This is where your pre-meeting review comes in handy to make them feel at ease, and important (by remembering details about them) right away.

2. Paint a picture of the next few minutes (or meetings). A great many customers walk into 'the sales meeting' anxious and on guard of being duped, and unsure of what to expect. Giving them a high level overview of what your meeting (or sales process) will entail helps them feel empowered and in control. This is right where your prospects want to be, which makes the process more enjoyable for them and earns you major relationship points!

3. Ask questions. As our survey in chapter 5 uncovered, our customers want us to ask them questions, and listen to and understand their needs before suggesting anything. As such, ask questions to ensure you understand their goals, their challenges, and the frustrations they have (or have had) in navigating a solution. Don't forget to ask them

personal questions too, as you read their comfort level in engaging with you. This help will help with our next step, which often happens simultaneously.

4. Build rapport. If you've followed the first three above steps, you're already there. Chapter three also helps to achieve rapport in mastering your body language, and your focus. If your focus is on your prospect, your body language will tell them that you are genuinely interested in them, not just their money. People want to be liked!

5. Insert your talking points or script. While people want more than just the product or service spec sheet regurgitated to them, they do want you to know what you're talking about ("be knowledgeable" ranked fourth on our survey, after all). The key here is to know your product or service, and your value proposition so well that it can come across conversationally, rather than robotically scripted.

6. Build value. Again, if you've followed the previous steps, you've already been building a lot of value for your future customer along the way. The key to driving home as much value as possible here is to connect the dots for them between their pain points, challenges, and goals – and your value proposition. This must not be manipulative, instead it should be conversational, educational, and affirmational (affirming you as their best choice).

7. Offer a trial or demonstration. This could be a free week trial for a fitness facility, or a 'first massage is on us' policy. It could also be the ergonomic office furniture sales representative who lets their prospect

have try-out their new office chair for a week before making a decision.

8. Get them to "yes" before the money comes up. You've probably done this already without knowing it. If you've been asking questions along the way as step three suggests, then chances are they've already said yes a few times. Using the above example of a free massage, perhaps the wellness center owner could ask a series of questions like,
- "Did you enjoy your massage with Jeff?"
- "Was your back less stiff afterwards?"
- "Do you think incorporating massage therapy into your routine would help with your posture and reducing pain?"

9. Break down barriers. Our win-win selling approach does not advocate for a long list of strategies to overcome customer objections. Rather, we suggest breaking down any remaining barriers to the sale before you ask. At this stage of the process, those barriers may be known or unknown. According to research, professionals with high levels of emotional intelligence make, on average, $29,000 more than those with low scores[35]. If you can take more of an empathetic approach, which is one method of tapping into your emotional intelligence[31], your listening skills are improved, and you'll have a better idea of the real and perceived barriers your prospect sees. Some of the barriers we hear are cost, which can be redirected into a conversation on value, or purchase decision authority, which can be made into a more collaborative process involving all parties. Timing, return on investment, and other potential barriers are important to meet head on and, as step eight suggested, get your prospect to a yes.

151

10. Get on the same page. When you've broken down the potential barriers, you can make sure that you and your prospect(s) are having the same conversation. You don't want to be talking value to a customer who is only hearing price. You also don't want to be talking urgency to a customer who is thinking intermediate to long term, or just kicking tires as the saying goes.

11. Ask for the sale. This may seem the most obvious piece of advice in the world for someone making a career in sales, but we are shocked at how often we see the most obvious step missed when we give sales talks, sit in on interviews, or consult business professionals. We have to learn to ask for what we want (in business and in life)! Pages 77 and 78 at the end of chapter five go through a number of different ways to ask for the sale if you are not 100% comfortable doing so at this point.

Post-sale Phase

We are firm believers that our work is not done after the sale. Even if our new customer or client is over-the-moon happy with our products or services, we want to create raving advocates, not just satisfied customers. To turn your customers into a virtual sales army for you, we recommend a few key post-sales activities.

1. Follow up. We've mentioned this a few times, and we dive into follow up further in the next chapter, but it's a can't-miss step. By following up to make sure

our customers are happy, we create a few more opportunities;

- We get the chance to ensure they are happy with our solution, rather than have any buyers' remorse creeping in.

- If they're really happy, they can often beat us to the punch with upsell opportunities or referral suggestions. "Do you sell (blank)?" or "I have a colleague who I think would benefit from your services" are often heard on a well-timed follow up call.

2. Contracts, purchase orders, and paperwork. Have you ever been super excited at a verbal yes, only to have your new deal dissipate before the bill was paid? This might seem like another obvious step, but we must be very timely with the delivery of contracts and paperwork after a yes to ensure their order goes through, and is ultimately fulfilled (especially if you are selling products that must be shipped from a fulfillment center in another state, province, or country).

3. Thank them! We can never take for granted that our customers have a choice when it comes to meeting their needs. They should know, and feel, that we appreciate their business. You might send a thank you gift and/ or card. You may opt for a heartfelt thank you phone call, or at least email. Depending on your budget and corporate policies, you might take your new client out to the theatre or a ball game. Whatever you do, never forget to thank them!

4. If they haven't offered, ask for a referral. This is a great step to have in your sales process, and not just because it can produce another sale for you. Would

you ever ask a client who wasn't happy for a referral? Of course you wouldn't. By having the referral ask step (even as subtle as, "I'm so glad you're happy Mark! Is there anyone else you know of that would value our services as you have?"), you're subconsciously forced to make sure your clients are happy. Even if your client doesn't give you a referral, they're more likely to stick around which lifts their customer lifetime value and your bottom line.

5. Always follow up after you do get a referral. When you do get a referral, it's absolutely imperative that you circle back with your customer (or colleague, vendor, etc) that gave you the referral to give them a status update and of course thank them. For instance, "John I just wanted to call to say thank you for referring us Candace! We had a great meeting, and she's still deciding, but I wanted to call and give you an update nonetheless. Thanks so much once again, and let me know if there's anything I can do for you!"
When you call John back (as a matter of urgent priority) it reinforces how referral-worthy you are – that you are a consummate professional, focused on taking expert care of all of your clients. John is more likely to refer you others, and even reach out to those people he's referred you that are deciding and give them a nudge for you. It works!

The final point we want to make on the sales road map, is to break down where you break down. In other words, as you read the above stages, you probably were giving yourself a mini self-assessment. If you know where you typically lose confidence or momentum in the sales process, you know where to focus to improve your process.

In their fitness experience, Lee and Stan had similar ways of increasing prospects' comfort during the most anxious part of fitness sales. Inevitably, prospects were given a tour of the gym or training studio, introduced to several team members, and then walked into an office.

It is at that moment – away from the high energy fitness floor and welcoming staff – that it's just them and you. You and your prospect – and a contract.

Conventional sales process would dictate a work flow process such that after the tour, you discuss options. When you follow such a protocol after moving your prospect from a welcoming environment to a quiet office with a contract in front of them, their energy changes – a lot!

Our authors came up with a different strategy. Instead of closing the door and discussing membership or personal training options and prices, they created a 'bridge conversation' that would overcome moving to a private office and closing the door.

By saying something like, "it gets very loud at reception, and I'd like to ask you some questions about your goals to make sure I can recommend the right trainer", the door could be closed in an act of customer service more than the prospect fearing, "Oh no, here comes the sales pitch!"

Break down your sales process as much as you can, whether you use a spreadsheet, Post-it notes, or a flow chart, and then start to assess how you (or your team) does at every critical juncture.

When we truly become students of the game, and artisans of our craft, we can consistently improve our results, the value we bring to our organization, and the compensation we earn as a result.

When we learn to improve every aspect of our craft, we truly learn how to sell in any economy. Our final chapter in this book covers how to adjust the fundamentals you have learned to shifting economic trends so that you can come out on top – no matter what (or when).

CHAPTER ELEVEN
Pages Into Points

❖ While every sale is unique, most sales follow a typical trajectory or set of stages.
❖ Understanding the goal of each stage, and the set of actions or deliverables you must take as a salesperson, are key to success
❖ The most successful sales professionals reflect on where they are strong, and where they can improve, throughout the process, and set out towards continuous improvement.

Chapter Twelve

Sell in Any Economy

Finally, we arrive at the crux of a rather bold, perhaps ostentatious, title for a book. We have seen, over the last 30 years, that it *is* possible to sell in *any* economy. As we discussed in chapter ten, our strategy must change, adapt, and evolve over time. With focus on key performance indicators (KPIs), we empower our business to become more agile as opportunities change, emerge, and evaporate.

In addition to measuring success and shifting to where ROI dictates, there are many tactical approaches and fundamentals proven to yield results. There are also ways to adjust to macroeconomic trends like a *bull* or *bear* market. Though not an exhaustive compendium, we'll cover each aspect of how to sell in any economy.

Sell in any economy

There are winners and losers in any economy, but one difference for those who win, regardless of what the market is up to, is **follow up**. According to HubSpot, it takes an average of 18 calls to connect with a buyer.[5] Furthermore, salespeople who follow up with a prospect within an hour after meeting were seven times more likely to have a meaningful conversation with a buyer or decision maker.[5] On the other hand, 55% of sales professionals did not respond to prospects within five business days![26]

Figure 11.1 below shows exactly why follow up is so important. With time, our prospects become distracted – they go back to their everyday lives. Regular (albeit respectful) follow up keeps us top of mind more often.

Figure 11.1: The Forgetting Curve

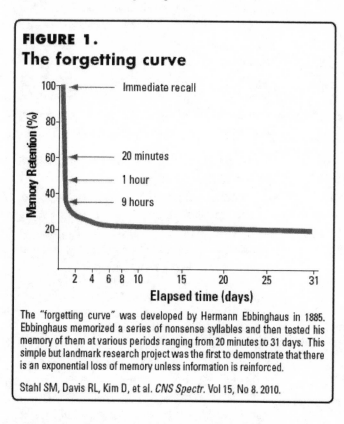

FIGURE 1.

The forgetting curve

The "forgetting curve" was developed by Hermann Ebbinghaus in 1885. Ebbinghaus memorized a series of nonsense syllables and then tested his memory of them at various periods ranging from 20 minutes to 31 days. This simple but landmark research project was the first to demonstrate that there is an exponential loss of memory unless information is reinforced.

Stahl SM, Davis RL, Kim D, et al. *CNS Spectr.* Vol 15, No 8. 2010.

Following up doesn't stop after the sale is made. Farmers are excellent at following up to ensure customer satisfaction, which keeps the customer in the doors and improves retention and customer lifetime value. Hunters should also be following up because 84% of all buyers now begin their process through a referral.[5] Furthermore, 83% of all customers would be happy to give a referral but only 29% end up doing so, and in most cases, it's because the salesperson simply doesn't ask.[5]

Sales professionals who are **resilient** also outperform their peers. One of the first lessons anyone hoping to pursue a career in sales or business ownership must learn is that "no" doesn't mean no to *you*. When we take "no" personally, we tend to react emotionally and beat ourselves up. Our confidence erodes and, as we discussed in chapter three, how you show up to every meeting is a critical component to your overall success.

In our experience, one of the best ways to mitigate the emotional reaction to the word "no" is to make more calls and set up more appointments. If you only have one sales meeting the entire week, your success hinges on that one potential sale. If you can achieve six or seven sales meetings per week, along with the top 5% of all performers[26], you become able to recover from a "no" much more easily. It becomes a numbers game, and, with enough input, your output starts looking pretty good! The average sales representative makes eight contact attempts[26]; those who go the extra mile and make 12 attempts perform, on average, 16% better in terms of sales.[26]

One of the most important things that those who can sell in any economy **do is focus on their customers**. They focus on their customers' needs throughout the sales process, and they keep those needs in mind afterwards. This may be a teenager who refuses to see a potential customer walking into a retail store as a distraction while working with their friend. It could also be a 36-year-old account representative, who takes the time to handle a customer concern rather than seeing it as a distraction from hitting targets. As our research showed in chapter five, focusing on our customers' needs is the key to sales success. Take care of your customers, no matter what, and you'll have customers – no matter when!

While there may be many more fundamentals to win customers in any economy, our fourth and final suggestion is to **keep learning**. Regardless of what the economy is doing, sales may be up or down for any number of countless reasons. The more we learn about our own (and competitors') products, our customers, our industry, industry trends or disruptive technology, the more prepared we become and more valuable to our business. The world is constantly changing, and through this change, the world is becoming more competitive. Our only hope is to change with the times and get a little better, and smarter, every day.

Selling in a robust economy

While it may seem that selling in a growing economy may be easy or automatic, there are inherent challenges to growth as well. For one, a booming marketplace attracts new competition. Larger markets or entire industries invite new B2B (business to business) services, and new disruptive technology. The smart phone, for instance, completely changed the cellular industry. Nokia, the market leader prior to the release of Apple's iPhone, saw their income drop at almost the same level that Apple's income rose![32] This was in a strong economy, happening within quarters, prior to the global economic meltdown of 2008.

There is hope, and there are things that you can do to protect your competitive advantage and reap the benefits of a strong economy. As Robin Sharma advises in *The Greatness Guide*, the more your company grows and the larger you become, the more important it is to be consistent with the little things that got you to where you are.[33]

Some of the best practices for thriving in a strong economy that we suggest are;

I.   Connect or reconnect with your customers. No one wants to be *just a number*. Reaching out to your customers as you grow goes a very long way in showing them how much you appreciate their business. It also demonstrates that your customer service isn't going to erode as you grow, which happens to many companies (who end up losing a lot of their customers to competitors who show them more appreciation).

II. Hold your prices steady as more opportunistic providers price gouge.

III. Reinvest your profits. This could be a business investing higher than expected profits into research and development for new products and services, or it could be a sales professional spending part of a large bonus on new books or courses to stay sharp.

IV. Form strategic partnerships to cater to larger customers or markets. The opportunity to level up often exists during a booming economy. A competitor or affiliated business may become an ally in your ability to combine services or products, and you're now able to satisfy new territories or larger corporate clients with larger budgets.

V. Make hay while the sun shines. Not every business sees a boom. Sometimes the selling summer is short, and it must be maximized while it lasts. Get busy taking advantage of the opportunities while you can!

Selling in a recession or economic downturn

While we must manage our budgets and conserve cash-flow and resources during a downturn, we must also show up in a way that instills confidence in our buyers. Research by Gulati, Nohria, and Wohlgezogen[34] shows that, while 17% of companies don't survive a recession, 9% of all companies come out of a recession stronger than ever! Their research concluded that companies who cut costs and focused on operational efficiencies, while still investing in marketing and research and development, fared better than companies that aggressively cut costs, or those who spent heavily on marketing.[34] This makes sense when we consider that prospective customers act from a top of mind perspective when shopping to fill a need. Advertising keeps your company (if not your specific product, service, or value proposition) fresh in your target audience's minds. When their budget recovers, they will turn to your company if you remain top of mind.

In addition to strategically reducing spending and continuing to invest in marketing, there are several other things a sales professional or business can do to sell in a downturn.

I.   "Portfolio yourself": If sales of your premium product or service start to wane, consider expanding your offering to include lower cost options. It's important to differentiate properly so that your full-fare paying customers don't trade down to a lower cost alternative. The key is to open new markets with an almost completely different offering, albeit related to your core business. This could be a boutique winery that (under a different brand) offers a high-volume wine as well.

II.   As in a boom, connect with your customers. In an economic downturn, they're going to reduce spending wherever they can. Reinforcing the personal connection is a great move, but the simple act of checking in also often serves to reinforce the value (even perceived value) your customers are getting from you.

III. Offer flexible options. During the global economic crisis of 2008, automobile companies were offering layoff protection. Sales were sliding as an entire nation worried for their jobs. To overcome a lack of consumer confidence, they offered return your vehicle at no penalty programs, or payment coverage campaigns in the event a consumer, who just purchased a new car or truck, found themselves to be unemployed.

IV.   Align what's best for you with what's best for the customer. Customers may start to shop on price when their budgets get tighter. Offering larger discounts with longer term contracts may be a great win-win; they get better pricing and you get a longer-term commitment and greater income predictability.

V.   Expand to new markets. Changing economic conditions create new challenges, but also new opportunities. Slowing housing sales for traditional detached homes may open a massive appetite for modular homes or condominium and apartment sales.

VI.   Follow the change in behavior. People still spend in a downturn, they just change how they spend. Instead of going out to nice restaurants and meeting friends at pubs, they may eat at more affordable restaurants, eat at home more often, and drink at home where it's much cheaper. While the fancy French bistro or the upscale steakhouse may suffer, the family restaurant may flourish. Pay close attention to your industry during the onset of a recession and you'll be better positioned to adapt your strategy to where your customers are now spending.

To close this chapter, we take you all the way back to chapter three. To sell in any economy, we must control our thoughts and beliefs. An athlete could never hope to make the Olympics on a steady diet of pizza and potato chips, just as we can't succeed in business on a mental diet of negative beliefs.

It's our hope that with the fundamentals, strategies and disciplines within your day, and within your mind that we've covered – you'll be empowered to succeed in any industry. It's our aim that you will have the tools to win in any economy.

If you believe in what you (or your company) does, and you truly care about your customer, plus you have the systems and disciplines proven to win, nothing can stop you – not the economy, the competition, nor anything. It might not be easy – adversity is all but a certainty – but it's more than possible.

We would go as far as betting on your success if you can choose a positive, winning mindset, and stick to the success principles we have outlined throughout this book. You may not win every customer, but you'll improve your input activities, which inevitably improve your output – your results.

Now go, prospect, systemize, follow up, and win! We wish you (and your customers) nothing but success.

CHAPTER TWELVE
Pages Into Points

❖ There are winners and losers in every economy. Companies can close their doors during a boom, or see record profits during a bust economy.

❖ The keys to selling in any economy always come back to focusing on the customer, and your business, in that order.

❖ If you truly know yourself, know your customers, and know your stuff – you will Sell In ANY Economy!

Appendix A: Summary of Sales Survey Responses

On the following page is the complete list of responses and their frequency from the North American Sales Survey mentioned in Chapter 6.

	Top Trends	%
1	Understand my needs	10.98%
2	Listen before suggesting	8.54%
3	Educate me	7.01%
4	Be knowledgeable	6.71%
5	Focus on my best interests	6.10%
6	Treat me with respect	5.79%
7	Low/ no pressure	5.18%
8	Be helpful	5.18%
9	Know your VP - how are you better?	4.57%
10	Be available, but not hovering	4.27%
11	Be genuine/ authentic	3.96%
12	Let me lead/ ask questions	3.66%
13	Be friendly	3.35%
14	Give me options	3.35%
15	Give me time	3.05%
16	Ask me questions	2.44%
17	Believe in your product	2.44%
18	Follow up	2.13%
19	Cater your approach	1.83%
20	Don't waste/ take too much of my time	1.52%
21	Show you care	1.22%
22	Don't lead with discounts	0.91%
23	Be prepared/ do your homework	0.91%
24	Be honest	0.91%
25	Be empathetic	0.91%
26	Be thorough	0.61%
27	Be reliable	0.61%
28	Be professional	0.61%
29	Validate/ justify my emotional purchase	0.30%
30	Maintain eye contact	0.30%
31	Be courteous	0.30%
32	Be clear/ concise	0.30%

Appendix B: Grow Who Know™ Workbook

Your Love Army™	Referral	Recep-tionist	Date & Method of Contact	Follow -up Date #1	Follow -up Date #2	Follow -up Date #3	First Mtg Date	6 Times, 6 Different Ways Over 6 Months

Acknowledgements

We would like to thank sales expert and bestselling author Daniel Pink for permission to use the research he gleaned in *To Sell is Human* to support the philosophical framework that we are all in sales.

We would like to thank the thousands who took part in our "How do you like to be sold to?" survey - your answers were pure gold!

We would like to thank the amazing, thorough, and patient Elli Townsend for editing our book and bringing us from the mildly coherent to the flowing novel you are reading today.

We would like to thank the brilliant Lindsay Jeans at Olive West Design Co. for the cover design and customer journey map infographic that are both amazing – and light years ahead of our collective skill set.

We would like to thank our most amazing clients who we have the privilege of serving and learning with – every day. You make us feel blessed to do what we do every day!

And last, but of course not least, we want to thank our families and friends for their support, patience, and understanding while we took what little time three entrepreneurs have for family – and instead used it to write this book! We love you and it is only because of your support that we can dedicate the time it takes to hone our craft.

Resources

1. https://www.ted.com/talks/simon_sinek_how_great_le aders_inspire_action Sep 2009, TEDx Puget Sound

2. https://www.businessnewsdaily.com/4173-personality-traits-successful-sales-people.html

3. Boundless. "Relationship Selling." Boundless Marketing Boundless, 26 May. 2016. Retrieved 8 Aug. 2017 from https://www.boundless.com/marketing/textbooks/bou ndless-marketing-textbook/personal-selling-and-sales-promotion-14/types-of-selling-93/relationship-selling-463-886/

4. https://hbr.org/2011/06/the-seven-personality-traits-o

5. . https://blog.hubspot.com/sales/sales-statistics

6. Alexander, Jessica Joelle and Sandahl, Iben Dissing. The Danish Way of Parenting: What the Happiest People in the World Know About Raising Confident, Capable Kids. 2016.

7. Pink, Daniel. To Sell is Human. 2013. Riverhead Books. NY, NY, 10014 USA.

8. Skorupski, John. The Domain of Reasons. 2010. Oxford University Press.

9. https://www.propellercrm.com/blog/sales-statistics

10. http://www.kaaj.com/psych/smorder.html

11. Wood, Wendy,Quinn, Jeffrey M.,Kashy, Deborah A. *Journal of Personality and Social Psychology*, Vol 83(6), Dec 2002, 1281-1297

12. Murphy, Dr. Joseph. The Power of Your Subconscious Mind. 5th Ed. 2000. Bantam Books.

13. Jensen, Peter. Thriving in a 24-7 World. 2015. iUniverse Books. Bloomington, IN 47403 USA.

14. https://www.nasp.com/article/A7EF5E14-7E28/setting-up-your-cold-calling-script.html

15. http://www.thesalesexperts.com/21-shocking-sales-facts-that-will-change-how-you-sell-forever/

16. Georgieva, Magdalena. https://blog.hubspot.com/blog/tabid/6307/bid/29757/lead-nurturing-generates-nearly-3x-more-clicks-than-email-blasts-data.aspx

17. Mawhinney, Jesse. https://blog.hubspot.com/marketing/7-effective-lead-nurturing-tactics

18. Pitts, Anna. http://www.businessinsider.com/only-7-seconds-to-make-first-impression-2013-4

19. https://thegogiver.com/dt_gallery/go-givers-sell-images/44-focus-your-curiosity-go-givers-sell-more/

20. http://blogs.umb.edu/quoteunquote/2012/05/08/its-a-much-more-effective-quotation-to-attribute-it-to-aristotle-rather-than-to-will-durant/

21. Durant, Will. The Story of Philosophy. 2012.

22. https://www.youtube.com/watch?v=Kjry--xWVZE

23. https://www.entrepreneur.com/slideshow/295677

24. https://getcrm.com/blog/sales-statistics/

25. https://customer.io/blog/timing-week-day-email-sending-schedule.html

26. https://www.onepagecrm.com/sales-statistics

27. Blount, Jeb. Fanatical Prospecting. 2015. Wiley & Sons. Hoboken, New Jersey.

28. Koch, Richard. The 80/20 Principle. 2008. Doubleday. New York, New York.

29. https://blog.hubspot.com/customers/how-to-design-your-sales-process-in-hubspot-crm

30. https://www.league.co.za/articles/companies-that-automate-lead-management-see-a-10-or-greater-increase-in-revenue-in-six-to-nine-months/

31. Bradberry, T. & Greaves, J. Emotional Intelligence 2.0. 2009. TalentSmart. San Diego, Ca.

32. http://www.businessinsider.com/chart-of-the-day-income-for-apple-nokia-motorola-rim-2010-9

33. Sharma, Robin. The Greatness Guide. 2006. Harper-Collins Publishers.

34. Gulati, R., Nohria, N., and Wohlgezogen, F. Roaring Out of Recession. Harvard Business Review. March, 2010 issue.

About the Authors

Lee Cassels

Lee Cassells is an experienced sales professional with over twenty years of experience in the 'business to business' and 'business to consumer' marketplace around the world. His role as a change agent has been positively received by his affiliates, whom hold him in high regard for his ability to achieve results. Lee's experience, drive and determination to "getting things done" has been the backbone of his success in the complete betterment of the organizations he has been a part of.

As a keynote speaker in the field of sales Lee has presented to sell out audiences for various business networks and non-profit organisations with the view of spreading his knowledge and expertise. Keen to assist others, Lee has created IT Clubs to provide systems & education to enable healthcare professionals to become their own boss and thrive in a competitive marketing place. Don't work for the boss. Be the boss!

When not creating pathways for others to succeed, you can find Lee with his family on Vancouver Island, Canada. From surfing in the winter to hiking the many mountains in the summer, Lee can be found taking full advantage of what Island life has to offer. Life is good!

https://www.linkedin.com/in/leecassells/

http://myitclubs.com/

Catherine Brownlee

Catherine is the President and CEO of CBI, where she brings over 30 years' experience in executive search and development, marketing strategies and networking around the globe, across all sectors. Her database of over 85,000 contacts demonstrates her capacity to motivate, build and achieve results. Her passion for connecting people and organizations, while nurturing objectives and maintaining focus, is her forte. She was recognized by her peers for this with an award for being among the top five Women of Influence in Calgary and a Paul Harris Award through the Rotary Club of Calgary, respectively.

Catherine is a recognized expert and speaker on the subject of industry strategies and advancements. She developed and regularly presents the popular seminar, "How to get the job of your dreams." She co-authored two bestsellers: the 2007 *Want to Work in Oil and Gas?*, and the 2018 *Cat's Tips to Get the Job of Your Dreams*, which reveals strategies for finding great jobs anywhere.

www.catherinebrownlee.com or 1-403-861-2001

Stan Peake

Stan Peake is an expert in human potential and business strategy. Founder of two businesses, Stan also bought into a third business that underwent a merge and acquisition. Today he still owns and operates InSite Performance Coaching Ltd., which helps values-based leaders dominate their industries while making a positive impact in their communities and our planet. Certified as an executive coach, corporate facilitator, and in cultural transformation tools, Stan helps executives and businesses become the best versions of themselves.

Stan is also the author of *BREAKthroughs in Success: How a Broken Back Healed a Broken Mind*, and co-authored *Swim Upstream: Unsubscribing to Conventional Wisdom*. His articles have also been featured in *Entrepreneur Magazine, Bizztor Media*, and in newspapers across Canada and the United States.

Stan speaks regularly on success strategies, leadership, sales, and organizational culture. Though he coaches clients across the world, Stan lives in Calgary, Alberta with his wife Maria; son, Chase; and dog, Zeke. When not working he enjoys exercise, travel, and arguing with his wife over their sports teams. He can be reached at www.insiteperformancecoaching.com

Connect with Stan

https://www.linkedin.com/in/stanpeake/

https://www.facebook.com/InSitePerformanceCoaching/